HANNAH

HANNAH

A NOVEL BY

Robina Salter

*For Nina with
Kindest Wishes
from the author,*

Robina Salter

M&S

18 April '95.

Financial assistance of the Canada Council and the Ontario Arts Council toward the publication of this book is gratefully acknowledged.

Canadian Cataloguing in Publication Data

Salter, Robina.
    Hannah

ISBN 0-7710-7902-8

I. Title

PS8587.A628H36   1986   C813'.54   C86-093234-6
PR9199.3.S348H36   1986

Typography and assembly by The Literary Service, Toronto, Ontario

Printed and bound in Canada by T.H. Best Printing Company Limited

McClelland & Stewart Inc.
The Canadian Publishers
481 University Avenue
Toronto, Ontario M5G 2E9

*This book
is lovingly dedicated
to
my husband and our family*

Another Hannah once wrote:
"The world needs not so much to be told
as to be reminded."
— Hannah More, 1745-1833

Chapter One

Hannah awakened early on this bitterly cold January morning, mostly because of the wild wind lashing away at the little white frame home. Hoping to return to the same deep slumber her husband Haim still enjoyed, she snuggled down deeper into the feather mattress, sharing the warmth of his long flannel nightgown.

She grew ever more wakeful, however, as the eerie voices in the wind called insistently around the house that was home to Hannah and Haim Holt, their son Daniel and Hannah's mother Morna.

Hannah raised her head and listened for what she thought might be three quick, soft knocks at the door. If it had been an hour or so later, anyone at the door would have pushed it open, called out Halloa and walked right in. Doors in northern Newfoundland were seldom locked in this era: one year before the island was to become Canada's tenth province. The year was 1948.

In her role as the local midwife, the comforter for the undoctored Steadman's Cove and the neighbouring hamlets along the coast, Hannah was accustomed to being called at all hours to deliver a baby, ease someone's pain, soothe someone's dying. Could it be a call from the Spekes — Noah and Emma — the Holts' nearest neighbours and dearest friends? Their daughter Lyddie was expecting her first baby in the spring. But it was probably too early for Lyddie who was, in her mother's words, still "improving" every day.

Without waking Haim, Hannah rolled out of the deep feather bed and wrapped a bright-blue dressing gown around her long slender body. She gazed down at Haim's rugged face partly covered by the quilt and partly hidden by his long, rufous-coloured forelock. As she lit an oil lamp, she could see his lips chapped from working in the wind and slightly parted as though he were about to speak. She looked lovingly at Haim with the protective compassion those who are awake reserve for those they love still far away in sleep.

Haim, like the other fishermen in Steadman's Cove, a hamlet in northern Newfoundland, savoured the extra sleep that came with winter, in contrast to summer when they often broke rest at two in the morning to make the most of the short season when the seas were free of ice and nets came up bulging with silvery-grey, flipping, flopping cod.

Hannah tucked the covers around Haim, her hand following a deep indentation on one side of his chest. It was the area where, fifteen years earlier in the Barton's Bight hospital fourteen miles to the north of the Cove, Dr. John Weatherton had removed seven of Haim's ribs in an operation called a thoracoplasty. The procedure, popular at that time, was designed to allow a tuberculous lung to collapse, rest and recover from the ravages of the disease.

It was during his convalescence that Haim had met Hannah, who was then working at the hospital as a nurse's aide. Haim was twenty-six. Hannah was nineteen and eager to move on to see the world of St. John's, Montreal, Boston and beyond. But Mother Nature, with her deft hand for changing plans, smiled on the couple whose masterful glands and some other mysterious alchemy nudged them on to an ever-deepening love and marriage.

Haim's parents had been drowned at sea when he was only two and so it was his lot to spend his childhood in a

Labrador orphanage. Haim had been in Barton's Bight only three months, trying his luck at fishing, when he came down with the rasping cough and the high fever of pulmonary tuberculosis.

From his meagre childhood Haim had surely learned to count every blessing. And so he allowed it was just his good luck to be in the Bight when he "took with the tubercle"; to be near a good hospital; and, above all, to be "walking out" with the beautiful, tall, fair Hannah. In the rock-bound village of Steadman's Cove, where he played the fiddle for the dances, Haim was known as a "merry man." He was never one to "hang his fiddle at the door," being as cheery one day as the next, unless Hannah crossed his will, and then he showed a flaring anger.

At the time when Haim took ill, tuberculosis was the scourge of families and sometimes entire villages. Its white banner often carried a death sentence. But it was accepted as just one more burden to be borne by the victim and shared by the neighbours who "undertook" for him or her — doing the work and caring for the family left behind. And when tuberculosis laid its cold, cruel, bony fingers on a child, it was everyone's torture.

In the northern reaches of Newfoundland TB was not spoken of in the same hushed, embarrassed, foreshadowing whispers as it was in other parts of the world. Nor was it linked with the patient's attitude toward life — thus creating a situation whereby the victim was unfairly punished twice: once through the process of the disease and again through the suggestion that he had brought it on himself.

Nor did the tuberculosis of the North carry anything of the genteel or romantic about it. Nothing of the aesthetic, contemplative look ascribed in the nineteenth-century novels to the tubercular who sought cures in the clear, high altitude of the mountains or down by the warm, succouring seaside of the Mediterranean.

Newfoundland did have its share of mountains, the Long

Range, for example, and it had seaside, rocky though it was, in great abundance. But it was to the sanitoria the tubercular made their pilgrimages. Along with like sufferers, they experienced the heightened passion, the quickened thought, the ruddy cheeks when the afternoon fever began. Some of its victims coughed, spat and sweated their way back to health. Others went on to the painful, suffocating death awaiting those whose lungs were progressively ravaged. Such were the days before effective anti-tuberculous drugs were available.

It was natural enough that when Haim was ready to leave hospital he should go with Hannah to the home of her widowed mother, Morna Burns. Haim and Hannah loved each other dearly and were married the following June when the circuit Church of England minister eventually came by in his boat. By then Hannah was four months' pregnant.

On this January morning as Hannah was about to answer the door, Haim lay in the deep sleep of exhaustion that always claimed him after a day of chopping wood and hauling it by dog team, along with a barrel of water pailed out of a hole punched through the ice formed over a stream.

Hannah shivered as the cold passed through her body. She drew her long, blonde hair, still loosely braided from the night before, out from under her collar to hang down her back like a thick, tawny hawser.

Quickly Hannah climbed down the ladder-stairway until she touched the stove-warmed linoleum of the kitchen-living room where she welcomed the rush of the warm air rising up against her long bare legs. In the semi-dark the stove's round lids were circled in a red glow from the coal banked to keep the fire alive through the cold night. Small, puffing sighs came from the stove as though it held a catch of creatures resigned to their fate of a fiery prison.

Hannah hurried through the kitchen to see who was at

the door. But no one was there. She smiled at the trick the wind had played on her as she turned to go back into the warmth of the kitchen.

Three small rooms fanned off the kitchen. One was the guest room, always ready to receive anyone who needed a night's rest. This room also housed the family bathtub, an enormous grey zinc sarcophagus used for the weekly baths.

In the second room slept her fourteen-year-old son Daniel, and that early dawn he was just as weary as his father, whom he had helped haul wood and water the previous day.

In the third room slept her mother Morna, now in her early sixties, who had been a midwife herself in her younger years. Morna's snores competed with the shrewish ticking of Haim's yellow clock.

The yellow clock sat on the mantel beneath a sampler whose cross-stitches spelled out God Bless This House. On one side of the clock stood a death's-head photograph of Morna's grandmother, who had come to the coast from England as a bride in the first half of the nineteenth century. On the other side of the clock stood a high glass dome covering a spray of waxy blue flowers and a long coil of golden hair. No one knew where the glass dome had come from. Nor the golden hair. But everyone knew the clock was Haim's very own.

Fifteen years earlier when he was but a new groom, Haim had sent to St. John's for a clock to grace his mantel. It was one of his few earthly treasures. Every morning without fail he held the clock facedown in the palm of his left hand, and with the thumb and remaining two fingers on his right, he wound the key.

Dr. Weatherton, known as "Dr. John" up and down the coast, had amputated Haim's first and middle fingers because of an infection often called "seal finger." The American doctor, who came originally from New England to work in the hospital at Barton's Bight, understood the illnesses peculiar to the fishermen. He believed the fingers became infected by a virus when they were plunged into the eye sockets of a dead seal in order to drag it from the ice pan back to a waiting sled.

Every morning, with his clock wound, Haim would look it straight in the face and smile. Then he would nod and say to anyone listening, "There be's another day, look." It was as though he were God giving the world another stay of time. In an uncertain, fateful era it was his way of measuring his days, as surely as did Hannah when she wrote in a daily diary, a kind of intimate pillow book into which she poured her deepest thoughts and feelings.

Most of the time Hannah took no more notice of the clock's ticking than she did of Morna's constant rocking back and forth. But there were other days when the ticking moved right inside her head, as though it were a metronome. These were days when Hannah saw the Cove as a kind of Plato's cave, where she lived in the shadows and reflections of others, and was restless to grasp and understand the meaning of her life. And there were moments when she wanted to hurl the whole ticking clockwork into the laughing grey Atlantic.

The clock ticked on as surely as the Atlantic wove itself into the fabric of the villagers' lives. As steady as the ticking of the clock was the sea's offering of fish to feed those who lived in Steadman's Cove.

Hannah hurried up the ladder-stairs and climbed back into the warmth of the big downy bed. She was just drifting off to sleep when once again she was certain she heard three distinct knocks. Was her mind playing tricks on her, or had she somehow heard in advance the same three knocks as if in precognition?

Quietly Hannah scraped enough frost from the window to peer out. By the pale moonlight she could see a dog team and komatik, the sled used to carry people, wood, water, seals and anything else to be transported during winter.

Once more Hannah went down to answer the door. The ticking clock told her it was half-past four. Closing the kitchen door behind her, Hannah picked her way through the inner porch cluttered with rubber boots, sealskin boots, boat fuel, dog mash, brine, twine and oilskin clothes. She opened the outer door to a sweep of ice-cold air and saw a young man standing shyly before her. Leaning toward him, Hannah smiled and whispered, "Come in now. In out of the cold."

The young man peeled off his cap and by the light of her lamp Hannah could see his pale forehead seeping sweat.

"I'm Tom Prynn from Abel's Eye, miss. You don't know me but my woman Angie knows you from afore. Now we're expecting our first baby. Angie took sick day 'fore yesterday. Baby can't get through. Hard pains, look!"

It always bothered Hannah that anything as natural as childbirth should turn into a sickness but sometimes it became a matter of life or death.

"They all say baby'll never get through the narrows in her hips — where she took with the rickets when she was a little girl. But there's talk of Dr. Weatherton in the nearby of Abel's Eye. Scatterplace along the trail I've left word that he's to go direct to the house. I only hope he's not already gone back up to the hospital in the Bight."

Hannah nodded her head sympathetically while the agitated man caught his breath.

Tom began again. "See, Angie has mind of a promise you made to her when she was but a child in hospital. Seems you promised you'd born her baby for her. Well, it looks bad. Two midwives are still there. Priest's been and all. Will ye come, Miss Hannah?"

"Of course I'll come. I remember Angie very well," Hannah said, placing a comforting hand on Tom's arm.

"Thank you, miss. But mind ye bundle up. It's some cold out there."

Grappling with the wind and the weather was nothing

new to Hannah. She knew that in less time than it takes to chop off a cod's head, the wind could suddenly drop and cause a sailor to sit becalmed, wrapped in a grey blanket of fog with all the hospitality of a boa's breath. More than once in her travels from one bedside to another, Hannah had known what it was like to be driven off the dog-team trail by a blizzard to spend the night in a wayside hut, locally called a tilt.

Patience was built right into the northern character. The Newfoundlanders often reminded each other that "the storm always knows what it's doing, where it's going." And they wisely respected its decisions.

Sometimes Hannah tried to imagine what it would be like if there were roads in the North. She pictured cars — the kind she saw when she had visited her half-sister Belle in Montreal — driving up and down a coastal road through Steadman's Cove. But this morning Hannah knew there was nothing for it but to brace herself for the cold journey and the challenge at the end of it.

Hannah smiled comfortingly. "I'll be dressed and ready in a few minutes. If the doctor's already gone, we'll take Angie up to him at the hospital. One way or another we'll manage. Would you wait in here in the warm while I dress?"

"Thanks, miss, but there's a dog's trace to be tightened and a slat that worked loose on my komatik on the way up. I'll go look after fixing things up and see you the once." And he let himself out into the moonlit dawn.

In her mind's eye Hannah pictured the day when messages would fly quickly up and down the coast. But as it was, in 1948, on that January morning when Hannah heard the knock at the door, no one ever knew when to expect a traveller back home again.

Many a watchful glance passed from a kitchen window across the cold, clean wintry horizon looking for the familiar silhouette of a dog team pulling a komatik with a wife or mother, a husband or son back home again from some snow-sped travels.

Later when the snows were melted, the ice drifted off the shores, and the blue seas of spring were once more sparkling with silvery needles of light, the same eyes at the kitchen window looked to the wharf for signs of the family boat bringing a loved one home from hospital or back from sealing on the whelping ice or perhaps a fortnight's fishing.

In those days before confederation with mainland Canada, one watched and waited. One listened too, for often messages were sent up and down the coast over the radio just after the evening news. But the radio's batteries had to be up to hear the vital messages.

Families would gather around the radio after supper, listening for that special message which linked them to the whereabouts of a loved one. So bound together were the villages in their struggle to survive the weather, poverty and illness, that news of anyone from the Cove was everyone's concern and rose from an honest caring. The evening messages might tell that Jake Richards was doing well in hospital, or Ky Henson would be home from Harge's Hole on the coastal steamer, or that Hannah Holt would be home "first chance" — meaning she would be home as soon as possible.

Now Hannah had a good ear for music and she cherished the moments when she could listen to classical recordings broadcast from London, England, but she also weighed up the justice of spending the radio battery on music against the inevitable moment when the family would be eagerly listening to the news and the battery would go dead with the newscaster's voice trailing off mid-sentence.

Whether there was a message for a family over the evening news or not, it was understood that all roads led to home and the absent member would return as soon as possible.

They might come on a passing boat, a coastal steamer, a dog team or, in the spring, on foot through the mud, melting snow or gorse, where each foot sank into springy, suctioning depths. These were the times — the seasons in between — when there was too little snow for dog-team travel and too much ice for a boat, when a man or a woman might have to travel fifteen or twenty miles on foot.

Indelibly etched in Hannah's memory was a sickening scene she had seen as a child: six men setting off on foot for the hospital, carrying a sick woman aboard a door serving as an improvised stretcher.

Hannah now hurried back through the kitchen, on her way to get dressed in the bedroom. She was passing Morna's room when she stubbed her toe on her mother's old rocking chair. "Oh, shoosh!" she said softly as she moved the chair out of her path.

It was the chair in which her mother rocked away her days, finding that the gentle to-and-fro motion seemed to ease the arthritic pains which some years earlier had brought to a halt her days as the midwife in the Cove.

Every day Morna rocked back and forth, from time to time rolling her heavily jelled hips from one side to another to ease the hot, gnawing pain. Her head, skewed slightly to one side from her stiff arthritic neck, gave her a peering, questing look. The searching look was intensified for Morna wore a pair of thick glasses prescribed after Dr. John and a visiting American eye specialist had removed her cataracts.

Morna traced the start of her crippling illness to one night when she went up the coast on a small ship to look after a child delirious with diphtheria. The night was dark as squid's ink and an ocean swell tossed the vessel up and down and then from side to side. Some of the passengers hung sickly over the rail, "feeding the gulls," as the saying went.

Suddenly a splintering crash ripped through the ship. Men, women and children were thrown to the deck, like chess pieces pitching off the board. The vessel began to list seriously to starboard side. On the port side Morna and the other passengers scrambled over the sides of the sinking ship and down into the grey lifeboats tossing below. Mercifully, the human flotsam and jetsam were soon picked up from the bone-chilling waters, their cries having been heard by a passing vessel.

Morna loved to tell the tale to Daniel, and he never tired of listening. "'Twas the beginning of the shootin' miseries in me joints and the h'end to me midwifin' days, sure. . ."

Hannah listened to Daniel's steady breathing. Nothing ever awakened him unless his beloved Gran'morna, as he called her, stirred in the night, and then he was by her side in a flash.

In many ways Haim and his mother-in-law Morna were more of a couple than were Hannah and Haim. Often they agreed in discussions. They finished each other's sentences. Sometimes one or both would pound a fist on the table and say, "I were just thinking the very same t'ing. The very same t'ing!"

Though there were moments when Hannah marvelled at the complexity of her family, most of the time she recognized the lessons each of the three could teach her.

She also understood that every village along the coast had its own distinctive colouring, customs and ways of dealing with each member. But they all shared a loving respect and responsibility for the elderly and the infirm. Disabled though Morna was, she still held sway over her household from her rocking chair. She held the reins, much as in a Japanese painting a man fishing from a small boat in one corner of the canvas holds his own power even in the face of enormous sweeps of sea and sky.

To an outsider Steadman's Cove might look like a backwater bay. But to those who lived there, the Cove teemed with drama. Its people shared each other's joys and sorrows. Each carried a lantern for the other's path.

Chapter Two

As Hannah went upstairs to dress, anxious thoughts raced through her mind as they always did when she was faced with a life-and-death dilemma. She recalled the day nineteen years earlier when little Angela was admitted to hospital with rickets, the result of a lack of vitamin D and sunshine. Her back was twisted like a young tree growing toward sunlight in a crowded jungle, her pelvis severely narrowed from the pressure of her hip joints. It was only a few days after she was admitted to hospital that Angie, her pale, freckled face framed in thick curly auburn hair, looked up into Hannah's face.

"Miss Hannie, my love, if I has 'ere baby, come born he for me. Say me ye will, Miss Hannie. Say me now!"

An outsider listening to the child of six talking to Hannah, herself only a girl of fifteen, would have thought the two were just playing a game, making girlish pledges to some distant, dreamy cause. But in Newfoundland, having a baby was enough of a certainty in a woman's life that Angie spoke of it when she was still only a child herself.

"Of course, Angie, I'll come to you -- if I'm anywhere near your whereabouts! Just you send for me!"

Hannah was now thirty-four and Angie was twenty-five, considerably older than most women in northern Newfoundland to be having her first child. But Angie had had trouble conceiving. Now she was having trouble delivering. Hannah pictured the gentle Angie cruelly locked in labour, her agonizing pains spending themselves fruitlessly against a deformed wall of bone. As Hannah contemplated this ominous scenario, an electrifying wave of outright terror shot through her body.

Hannah shivered as she threw off her warm night clothes and put on panties and a bra made of fine, sheer, shimmering silk, the delicate colour of the inside of an eggshell. The lingerie was made from World War II surplus parachute silk and had come as a gift from her half-sister Belle in Montreal.

Twice a year Belle sent cartons of clothing back to the Cove, clothing which Hannah and her mother shared with the other women.

Once Belle had taken Hannah on a glorious shopping romp through the fashionable Montreal stores, but Hannah could not muster any enthusiasm for her new wardrobe.

"None of it feels like me, Belle dear," Hannah protested.

"Oh, come on, Hannie, it's great fun shopping. When I buy clothes, I feel as though I've just been made love to. Really."

Hannah wanted to tell Belle that for her no amount of new clothing could ever be a substitute for the warm, embracing love of a man.

There were other touches in the homes almost as paradoxical as Hannah's wispy lingerie, and almost always the items were gifts from a relative gone out from the coast, gone to find work on the mainland and remembering the folks back home with a memento.

Sometimes the reminder of someone "away" took the form of a tea towel with the letters BOSTON printed across one end. Or the souvenir might be a satin cushion with NIAGARA FALLS splashed boldly across its shiny middle.

In some homes the place was still set for each meal with the person's chair drawn up, as though he or she were about to walk in the door. The absent person's jacket might be hung over the back of a chair, with his mitts lovingly laid on either side of the dinner plate, alongside the knife and fork.

Dressed in her heavy clothing, Hannah took up a stout black comb and swept her long, thick, honey-coloured hair up into a mass on the crown of her head, where she anchored it with amber hairpins. Her mirror was a piece of highly polished metal which Haim had found on a ship wrecked on a nearby shoal.

In the moonlit dawn the reflection of Hannah's metallic mirror gave a soft glow, adding a gentleness to the fine features of her oval face. Her full forehead dipped to a recess between her large, violet-blue eyes fringed with dark lashes and framed above by fine fair brows the colour of her hair. Her nose was straight and narrow save where it flared slightly at the nostrils. But it was her full and sensuous lower lip, the half of a mouth that smiled slowly and generously, which saved her face from the severity of the nose and the lean, spare sweep of her jawline.

Glass mirrors were not a plentiful item in the Cove. Full-length mirrors were scarcer still. Anyway, no one took his appearance seriously. And anyone who was "struck on his looks" was soon taken down a peg or two by his neighbours. In the Cove, with its sixty souls, everyone was a neighbour and a face was studied more for the image of God shining through than for anything else.

Hannah was a young adolescent when she first saw herself naked in a full-length mirror. At that time she was visiting Belle in her Montreal mansion. One morning after a shower she looked at herself nude in a massive mirror covering one entire wall of the bathroom. Rising from a pink shell of a bathtub, she saw the reflection of her long, slender, glistening-wet body, more woman than child, looking back at her.

At first she turned away shyly from the sight of herself. Then she gazed again in a childish wonder, maybe even in confusion at seeing herself against the background of the luxurious marble bathroom, looking like the woman in Botticelli's painting "Birth of Venus."

That morning, as though by instinct, Hannah stepped back into the shower and turned a sudden downpour of ice-cold water on herself. In so doing, she was suddenly plunged into a different, mysterious world, with the torrent of cold water carrying her to a distant realm in her imagination where she was neither a curious questing adolescent nor the young woman who laboured on the coast with her mother and the other women.

Like the rest of the women, Hannah had had little time to think about her looks. The girls turned into women at an early age and were soon partners with the men in the struggle for survival. What a woman's body looked like was often considered more an accident of fate. And it was taken for granted that toil and childbirth would, in their time, take their inexorable toll.

What did matter was a woman's ability to survive and endure the often exhausting, repetitive physical labour, a monotonous and inadequate diet, and to hold to the prayer that the fish market would surely improve, that there would be an end to the nightmare of tuberculosis and the other ills often spawned in the pools of privation. Above all, they held to their faith that the Lord would provide. To the rhetorical question in the old maritime hymn, "Will Your Anchor Hold in the Storms of Life?" the answer was always a resounding "Yes!"

As the water poured over her that morning, she felt herself growing toward a new Hannah. She did not understand the process through which a sudden outpouring of cold water could lead her to understanding the power of herself as a woman, but she was to know that the same phenomenon happened every time she stood under a chilling deluge in Belle's shower.

With a shy wonder the young Hannah looked in the mirror at her high, round breasts, long, lean torso and slender legs. She knew it was the same body that carried mash to the dogs, stacked and turned the cod and often walked with her mother on her way to comfort the sick, "born" the babies or lay out the dead. It was the same body, but on that morning Hannah saw herself in a different light.

Hannah was at peace for another reason: just the evening before, Belle had provided the answer to the girl's poignant longing to know who her father was. Now, thanks to Belle, the young Hannah understood why she was taller and fairer than most of the other Newfoundland women.

As she reached for a large pink towel, the sudden cold kiss of a nipple against her arm sent a shiver through her body. Her coral-coloured nipples tightened into small nubbins of pain. Looking down at her fair triangular place of pleasure and procreation, she slowly wrapped herself in the warm luxurious towel.

As soon as Hannah was old enough to realize she had been conceived after the death of Walt — Morna's husband and Belle's father — she began to ask her mother who her father was.

Just the week before going to Montreal, Hannah had knelt before her mother, paring calluses from the woman's feet and tending what Morna called her indoor toenail. Suddenly she riveted her mother's attention.

"Now just who was my pa? I've a right to know. I'm as much his daughter as yours!"

Morna's eyes fled for refuge through the window to the boats riding restlessly at anchor. Her foot twitched in Hannah's hand and she cleared her throat. "Oh, he were jest a man from away, my doll. Jest a man from away."

And young as she was, Hannah understood that pain

and fear of criticism kept her mother from answering her question.

Belle, who had changed her name to Isabelle when she married Delbert Simpson, was more forthright. "There's no reason for you *not* to know that your father was a tall, handsome Swedish sea captain. He put into the Cove for one week during a series of bad storms. But *you'd* never hear that from anyone in the Cove. Back there what matters is the kind of person you are."

Hannah knew that a love child was amiably absorbed into a family. It might be another mouth to feed, but it was also another pair of working hands. And in any official census-taking, such a child was nimbly accounted for with a smile, a knowing nod and the quick reply, "Oh, his aunt had he, uh — down on the Labrador!"

On knowing who her father was, Hannah gazed into space. The speculative part of her became a reality. Something flowed free within her even though she knew she would probably never be called Aunt Hannah — in the familiar endearment used on the coast — the way her mother was Aunt Morna and her husband was Uncle Haim.

As Hannah tied the laces at the top of her sealskin boots, preparing to travel to Abel's Eye for Angie Prynn's delivery, she thought of Belle with gratitude for many things, including the cashmere socks she drew over the boot tops. She was especially grateful to Belle for telling her about her father. Like Morna, Belle knew the compelling attraction of "a man from away," a man whose ship was riding at anchor, just as Delbert's was one earlier summer. . . .

Belle was little, dark and daring. She had Hannah's mental ability, but she gave her thoughts their freedom more quickly. Words darted off Belle's tongue in shimmering shards that either lighted up a conversation or dropped it dead mid-air.

Belle met Delbert Simpson one summer evening when she

was strolling with her girl friends along a rocky path down by the water's edge. Delbert and his crew were standing at the rail of a smart white ship belonging to Delbert's family company. It was anchored in the Cove for ten days. With the easy cavalier manners of those who can glide out to sea again, the crew invited the girls aboard for dinner. Belle was invited back for dinner each of the ten nights while *The Golden Wish* rode seductively back and forth at anchor.

To Delbert, Belle had all the saucy freedom he could never quite grasp. While his father lived, Delbert, an only son, had moved under the stubborn thumb of the wealthy old man. Now he knew the shadow of his mother's diamond-heavy hand and her bracelet of golden charms tinkling like a cash register.

The last night *The Golden Wish* rolled in the waters of Steadman's Cove, Delbert took Belle in his arms in the quiet, steamy intimacy of his cabin. She closed her eyes against the sailing trophies banked across one wall and felt the strength in his long muscular arms taking over for her, becoming her energy, her power. He laid his cheek on her long dark hair falling over his arms. That night they spent themselves again and again. They lay cradled in each other's arms, rocking gently as the ship rolled at anchor and the dawn came up and spread its rosy glow over the still waters of the Cove.

Awakening to the sound of the waves gently slapping the side of the ship beneath their porthole, Belle started to jump up, but Delbert reached out and drew her down to him. He held her mouth to his and kissed her, his fingers wandering through her thick dark hair until she felt that her whole body was contained in his touch. By then it no longer mattered to Belle that her mother would be filled with anger. She had given herself to this man and there was no turning back.

As though he read her thoughts, Delbert eased her gently

down on her back, drew the covers over her against the cool air of the early morning and propped himself up on one elbow to gaze on her face.

"I want to see you again, Belle. We haven't talked long enough to know each other very well, but I know I want you. If you want me, then I'm coming back to take you out to Montreal to marry you before freeze-up. You have my word."

"I'll be here. I may work in St. John's for the summer, but I'll be here come fall."

And so they exchanged their early vows.

As Hannah tied a red scarf around her face, ready for the journey to Angie's bedside, she remembered how on that earlier morning Belle's hair had drifted loosely over her shoulders. Her skin was waxy and white, her eyelids were heavy, languid with love. She had the white, wan look women often have after making love or labouring in childbirth.

Belle knew that if she had spent the night with a boy from the Cove, Morna would only have busied herself with stirring the dog mash or kneading the bread. But Belle had stepped out of caste, cheapened herself in Morna's eyes by "mingling with the gentles."

Morna faced Belle, her loaf-like face ruddy and shot through with the same little red veins that track through a peach or the petals of a flower.

"Ye're turnin' yer back on heaven, sure. 'Tis to wear scarlet bloomers, look!"

"But I love him, Ma, I love him," Belle had protested.

"How could ye think ye've fallen in love with a man ye've known but a few days?" the mother asked. "How could. . ." Her voice trailed off, for had she not done the same thing with Hannah's father?

"He's comin' back to collect me afore freeze-up, Ma. We're going to marry in Montreal."

Leaning against the warming oven of the stove, Morna looked down at the brown linoleum, her head to one side as though she were listening to a memory speaking. She thought of her own night of love aboard a ship, the pain when it pulled away from the Cove, and she longed to spare her child the anguish she had known. But she knew in her mother's heart that often there was little one generation could teach another about life, about love.

Then the mother looked up at Belle and smiled, a sweet, wistful smile.

"Love takes some women quick-like. I know it took me once quick. With Hannah's pa." Morna sniffed, sighed, straightened up and changed the subject.

True to his word, Delbert Simpson came back before freeze-up. During the summer months, Belle had worked as a shop-girl in St. John's, spending her money on clothes, on getting her teeth set right, on a course in dieting and deportment. She walked with a new bearing. One day she bought her mother a new dress and a girdle to replace her old creaking "stays." And she gave Hannah a stack of diaries, onto whose blank pages the eleven-year-old turned her imagination loose.

Belle and Delbert were married quietly, much to his mother's dismay. Old Mrs. Simpson had hoped for a Montreal girl — with connections — and a large, billowy, newsy wedding. But Delbert had married the plucky, independent Newfoundland girl to help him remove himself as far as possible from his mother's control.

Hannah shifted the red scarf away from her mouth and smelled Belle's perfume, for her sister had worn the scarf the winter before when she and Delbert were skiing at the Simpsons' Laurentian chalet.

Hannah checked in the delivery bag again. It was the bag in which her mother had carried the herbs, simples and the barks and leaves for healing. Morna was convinced she could cure a toothache or a wart by a charm. Once she charmed a man's bleeding leg by tying a length of green worsted around his arm. Another time Morna charmed a woman's rheumatic pains by tying a haddock's bone, sewn into a little bag, around her neck. She crooned to those in agony as though the vibration of her voice could carry away another person's pain.

Morna could not, however, relieve her own rheumatic pains. "I needs someone to work the spell fer me. I needs a facilitator," she said, using a fancy word to weight her remarks toward Hannah.

But there were times when Morna herself wavered in her ministerings, her chantings, for her world was already moving away from the realm of fairies, boo-darbies and the spheres of the unseen, as Newfoundland glided from the age of the dog team toward the age of the jet.

At the same time Hannah knew as well as her mother that often the best and only therapies were kindness, prayer and the healing touch they both possessed.

Hannah had never looked back with any bitterness at the death of her first baby, a little girl called Amity, who died after a long and painful delivery where her mother and Emma Speke officiated. No, she did not look back in bitterness, but she approached every birthing bed with a new regard for the unexpected and often dangerous turn a seemingly simple delivery could take.

The day she watched from her bedroom window, through a double prism of tears and cold November rain, while Haim and a dark twist of men from the Cove carried Amity's tiny coffin up for burial on the Point, she resolved she would go to hospital for her next baby.

It was on just such a cold January fourteen years earlier when she had set off with Haim to the hospital at Barton's Bight for the birth of her second child. During a bitterly cold and perilous journey by dog team over bumpy trails in a lurching coach box, the komatik and coach box struck a snow-covered tusk of rock, hurling Hannah into the snow. By the time they reached the hospital, her unborn baby's heart was weak, and in desperation Dr. John delivered Daniel by caesarean section. The baby was blue at birth and took a long time to breathe spontaneously. Daniel was born a little "behind." But he was not so slow that the women ever asked Hannah if she had entertained bad thoughts during her pregnancy, or denied a craving, or looked upon a black cat.

Hannah and Haim accepted the boy without comment. He was nearly two years old before Hannah drew to Haim's attention what she had known almost from birth, but Haim was not willing to acknowledge it.

Before hurrying out to join Tom Prynn, Hannah wrote a note to her family: "Gone to Abel's Eye to deliver Angie Prynn. Coming home first chance. Love, H.H." She turned to pierce the note through one of the needles in a sock Daniel was knitting for his father. The boy was the only one of the trio who could read with any ease. But Hannah thought again and, walking across the kitchen, she propped it up against the little yellow clock, where Haim would find it when he wound up the minutes for another day.

Then Hannah strode out into the cold dawn, closing the doors quietly behind her. For a second she shivered from the bitter cold and fear of what she might find with Angie Prynn. Would the baby make its way into the world or would she have to bundle Angie into a coach box to make the dangerous journey to Barton's Bight?

When Tom saw Hannah running toward the sled, he brought the dogs into order. Hannah climbed onto the brown blanketed box lashed to the slats of the komatik, while Tom pulled back hard on the runners until she was secure. Then he gave the dogs their head. They pulled away with a jerk that almost sent Hannah over the back of the komatik as they set off at top speed for Abel's Eye.

Chapter Three

Tom and Hannah sped through the biting cold looking like two masked travellers. Only their eyes peered out between their toques drawn down low on their brows and their scarves wrapped around their noses and mouths to prevent frostbite to their faces.

It was a hungry wind blowing that January morning, sucking human breath to itself and easing off only long enough to catch its own breath again. It whistled through the spindly trees and across the snow-quilted barrens.

Tom hurled his long leather whip out high above the backs of the dogs with a crack that sent them flying on their way and with a skill that brought the entire length of it winding back to him like a trained snake.

"Hodie, hodie, hodie!" he called out to the lead dog, directing it to turn to one side, or "Keepaw, keepaw, keepaw!" when he wanted the team to pull the other way. As they passed through the village, Hannah noticed that all the houses were in darkness save for the green frame home of Ky and Twyla Henson.

Ky was the lay preacher in the Cove on those many Sundays when the itinerant, ordained clergyman was in another parish on his circuit. On a Sunday Ky would stand up in the pulpit of the little Anglican church, flailing his long, thin arms through the air and fanning them dramatically past his wiry, grey beard as he inveighed about the heat of Hell, the sins of the flesh and the spirit, and the punishment that follows greed, pride and failing to tell the truth.

Ky officiated at baptisms, weddings and funerals — from cradle to coffin in the chronology of the human lifespan. Sometimes he invited a bride for what he called a "heeding session." But no bride ever revealed beyond a giggle and a blush what went on in the guidance hour.

Twyla Henson helped her husband find the material that packed his Sunday sermons. Every week she cast a wide social net out over the Cove, seining in nibbles of news.

Twyla's sister Sadie operated a similar network at Barton's Bight, where she worked in the post office, receiving and sending telegrams as well as monitoring the messages to be sent out over the evening radio news. What one sister did not know, the other did.

Seeing the light in the Henson home, Hannah made a mental note to call in on her return. She had noticed one recent Sunday that Ky preached with an ever-rising wrath; his cheeks were flushed and he was short of breath. Hannah thought how gaunt had grown his tall frame and she wondered if perhaps Ky was joining the rising numbers of those fallen victim to the scourge of tuberculosis.

Tom ran alongside the dogs now, urging them to speed up as the komatik glided onto the main trail leading to Abel's Eye. It was a trail that wound around behind the foothill of a magnificent height known as the Point.

It was to this high windy Point overlooking the great, majestic churning ocean that Hannah ran whenever her tasks in the Cove eased up. She lived for the hours when she could walk out through the village and climb to the peak of the Point, an ancient formation of granite brushed to a high rough roundness by the swivelling tusk of glaciation. Up on its heights Hannah welcomed the sweeps of wind which fanned her own "inner winds" — those authentic personal blueprints and compelling elements within her: talents, gifts, drives, longings which when thwarted or denied could dwindle into a sickness of the mind and body.

From the Point Hannah would look back at the Cove and her concerns would become as dwarfed as the far-off houses, the boats and the harbour.

She had first gone alone to the Point as a child of eleven. Before that, she used to gaze out from her "play pen," a large barrel cut in half. She was safe in the barrel, in the salty hours when her mother worked with the other women at the fish stages, laying out and turning the previous day's catch.

Little Hannah's eyes just cleared the edge of the barrel, barely enough for her to peek out on the solemn procession of fishermen walking back and forth at the water's edge, emptying their boats of fish, then chopping off the slippery grey heads, splitting their bellies and clearing away the guts.

Hannah would then turn her gaze from the labouring men to feast her imagination on the Point. When she tried to make her escape from the barrel, the women, exercising a collective concern they felt for every child, warned her about the dangers lurking at the water's edge.

"Ooh, ooh, my little maid," they chuckled. "There be's the waterman out by t'water and he could spirit ye off forever!"

When Hannah was older she took her place beside the women at the long, wooden fish tables. Nothing gave her more pleasure than to finish her work and take off to the Point, where she could listen to her own inner gypsy thoughts rather than the endlessly cheery chatter of the women.

The local women liked to tease Hannah, to ask her if she had a "friend-boy" she was planning to meet out on the Point. They chided Morna for letting her young daughter climb to what they thought was a terrifying height.

Strict though she was in many ways, Morna understood her daughter's need for freedom. The mother knew that to stifle the girl's spiritedness, her daring, was to stymie her mettle and frustrate her inborn pluck.

In those early years Hannah restrained herself until she was out of sight of the women, wearily wiping their hands on their aprons and dragging themselves to their homes to begin another round of work: cleaning, laundering, sewing, weeding the garden and making the evening meal. Then Hannah ran to the Point as fast as her long, coltish legs would carry her — much as a child in a city or town might run toward the sound of a distant band with its pipes and drums heralding a day of holiday from school, a day to head for the meadow and the brook.

She would take in a deep breath of the ocean air, sit on a soft mossy patch, wrap her long arms around her legs and rest her chin on her bony knees. While the wind played with her long, silky hair, she would fix her gaze on the sea. Often she fantasized about her father as she watched the waves playfully pushing each other up on the shore.

Sometimes she imagined her father might have sailed right past the base of the Point in a long, dark Swedish ship. Other times she pictured him in a spotless, white vessel pulling into a warm, exotic, spicy island with palm trees waving a welcome to him. Often she dreamed of herself when she would be grown and grand. She pictured how she would stroll through long, elegant rooms painted pale yellow, talking of books with men who were tall and urbane, who wore white shirts with cuff links and laughed from hearts free of fear.

As she grew to womanhood, it was at the Point that Hannah felt the winds blow on the raw nakedness of her own sensuous nature. After the death of Hannah's first baby, Amity, Morna lost her capacity for sympathy toward

Hannah's almost ritualistic flights to the Point.

"'Tis right morbid of ye to keep runnin' out to the cemetery, chasin' after yer dead baby. Right morbid," Morna said, addressing her words more to Haim, as though Hannah were not quite present.

Haim was just as exercised as Morna about Hannah's fugues to her freedom, but not wanting Daniel to hear, he reserved his comments until they were in bed.

"Mind ye stop making they treks to the Point, Han. One day you'll fall clear off the cliff. We'll all be looking around for ye and there ye'll be — clean gone — into the sea!"

Haim's other concern lay in his fear that one day she might show Daniel the splendour of the sea from the Point and that Daniel, with his awkwardness and poor balance, might fall off the high cliff.

"If ye were ever to take Dan'l out there, mind, I couldn't say what I might do, Hannah. Can ye not find other ways to peacify yerself? Why can't ye be the same as the other women with things to do in the house that make them feel right content?" Like most of his fellow fishermen on the coast, Haim believed that all women were born with innate talents for sewing and knitting and for rearing their children.

Hannah heard Haim out patiently. It was a test of her tolerance because although Haim understood some of Daniel's physical and psychological limitations, he did not spare the boy the ignominy of losing his balance on a tossing boat whose deck was slippery with fish guts. The injustice and lack of logic made Hannah look forward all the more to the day when she would walk with Daniel to the great promontory that was her citadel and her cathedral, her place of wisdom and insight.

It was true that Hannah visited her baby's grave whose modest perimeter was marked with bits of shells she had gathered from the littoral. Every spring she emptied the shells — mostly clams — of their wintry meltwater and laid them in place again. She pulled away last summer's grasses, clinging like dead hair to the little white stone which bore the dates:

Born 9 November 1933
Died 11 November 1933

Then she brushed aside some weeds to reveal the white, concrete bouquet of baby hands reaching up to a stone angel whose wings spread out over the words: *Amity Holt —With Him, which is far better.*

Belle had sent the gravestone from Montreal.

Now with the Point well behind the dog-team travellers, Hannah scanned the horizon for a glimpse of Dr. John making his way back to Barton's Bight. She longed to see his familiar form, knowing she would need his help with Angie. On the climbs up the hills, Hannah jumped off the komatik to lighten the load for the dogs. She welcomed the exercise. Pounding one sealskin-clad foot after the other on the hard snow helped to ease the anxiety knotting in her stomach as they came closer to Angie's bedside in Abel's Eye.

Every village along the coast had its own tempo, its own ways of governing itself. And even though villages might be only a few miles apart, they differed from each other in small ways the inhabitants themselves were unaware of most of the time.

The village of Abel's Eye, only eight miles south of the Cove, was not a place Hannah visited regularly for it had two midwives of its own, as well as a priest. The last time she was in Abel's Eye she had gone down with Dr. John on the hospital ship to help immunize the school children. But it was not on Hannah's regular route.

Hannah grew up considering childbirth to be as natural as breathing. By the time she was twelve, she could almost have delivered a baby herself, so often had she sat in someone's kitchen — occasionally peeking through a door jamb into a bedroom where her mother was delivering a baby. In fact, by the time Hannah was fourteen, she had seen more of living and dying than most people see in a lifetime.

The mother, short and dark, and the daughter, tall and fair, were a familiar sight walking through the Cove. Morna always wore the same black felt hat with its brim rolled parallel to her thick black brows. The crown of it rose up high and round. It was a belvedere of a hat, a moving beacon for those waiting at a window for the sight of the comfort that came with its wearer. That derby of a hat had arrived many years earlier in one of the clothing bales from the mainland. When Hannah was little, she used to trace with her fingers the letters on a label inside the brim. And when she was old enough to read, she recognized the words *Made in Paris* embroidered into the black silk lining. In those simpler days Hannah would play with the children in someone's kitchen until they heard the newborn's cry, and then they'd wait for the moment when her mother called, "Well, come on in and see the new baba!"

Tom and Hannah were nearing the village now with still no sign of Dr. John. As though Tom read her thoughts, he looked around at Hannah. He had turned his cap backward to streamline himself and so cut down on the wind resistance. When he smiled at Hannah, his lips parted like curtains to a cast of broken, missing teeth — all out of character with his fresh, young skin. Hannah and Belle had Morna to thank for their good teeth and sound bones.

Once or twice a week Morna made a brew of cod's liver and served it to the girls on bread with margarine and molasses. On such days they would come home, sniff the air and say, "Ma's manging up the livers again!"

"We'll be there the once now, look!" said Tom.

"'Tis on the downhill now!" Hannah said, trying to match his attempt at optimism.

The lavender light of the earlier dawn was now a rosy haze coming from an ominously red sun dragging itself up over the homes of Abel's Eye. Hannah remembered the outporter's poetic aphorism:

Red sky at night, sailors' delight.
Red sky in the morning, sailors, take warning!

The small frame homes, painted yellow, white, green and blue, were set at odd angles to each other as though they were large wooden blocks kicked by the hapless boot of a passing giant to land where they may.

At the sound of the snow crunching crisply under the komatik's runners, the local sled dogs stirred in their outdoor pens. First one dog stood up and raised his head to howl a private proclamation to the heavens, as though to alert the village that strangers had arrived. Then the other dogs throughout the village joined the primitive cacophony and one lace curtain after another stirred in curiosity as the village awakened to the sound of the midwife's arrival.

"Now I'm off to the narrows to see if doctor's been there or where he might be. I'll be back the once. Good luck to ye," Tom called as the dogs drew away under the menacing sound of his whip cracking through the air.

"We'll do our best," Hannah called to him as she steeled herself to walk up the icy path to the Prynns' door. She knocked and let herself in, glad to be out of the cold. Her nostrils were assaulted with a rush of warm, stale air carrying the smells of stagnant humanity and oil lamps burning themselves out. The two elderly local midwives, dressed entirely in black, sat dejectedly beside a long grey stove.

"Good morning," Hannah said respectfully, aware she was treading on their rather tenuous territory.

The midwives nodded to Hannah in unison as though they shared one central nervous system.

"How is Angie this morning?"

The midwives glanced sideways at each other to see who should speak first. Their faces had that greyish hue that comes with fatigue and failure. One looked down at her hands, the fingers interlocked, the gnarled thumbs making circles around each other. The other one looked over at Hannah.

"There's nothing more to be done, Mrs. Holt. Father Machovie's been to give her the last rites. 'Tis in the Lord's hands now. 'Tis." And the women settled back into their collective blackness. They were like two brooding hens momentarily ruffled by a passing hawk.

Just then Angie called out in a thin, tired voice from a room off the kitchen. "Hannie, I'm in here, do come in."

Hannah picked up her midwife's bag and hurried toward the room. A large gilt-edged mirror covered part of one wall, rivalling the wallpaper with its full, overblown red roses, their petals bruised and bluish-looking, their stamens reaped of pollen. A statue of Mary with the boy Jesus on her knee stood on top of a small pine dresser. Angie lay passively like a slender stem with a gall bulging out on one side.

"I'm some glad ye've come, Hannie, some glad!" She looked intently into Hannah's face, then nodded. "Ye're just the same Hannah. Just the same Hannie I knew all they years back."

Hannah took Angie in her arms and held her with the tender love and understanding one woman feels for another who is an innocent victim of tragic circumstances. She felt Angie's frail and exhausted body in her arms and then she eased her back to look into her eyes.

Something raw and rebellious rose inside Hannah at the sight of Angie trapped like an animal in a painful vise. She felt angry for the rugged and ragged life meted out to those women who suffered helplessly. And for a moment Hannah felt frayed like a rope on too fast a passage through a whirling pulley. "I'll be back in a moment, Angie," she said, and went out to the kitchen where she cheered on the midwives to make tea for them all. Opening her bag, she took out her white sugar sack apron and tied it around her middle. Three large blue X's and the word *SUGAR* marched jauntily across one of her hips and a square bib covered her breasts.

The local midwives were part of the drama again and they sipped their tea in the bedroom while Angie's futile contractions came and went without any results. But Hannah's spirit rose in steady hope.

"Angie, my love," she said, "there are things to be done. I believe that before the sun sets there's going to be another little person in this family and it's not someone coming in through your front door either. Will you believe that with me, Angie Prynn?"

Angie nodded but seemed unconvinced. She felt herself moving toward the place already reserved for her in paradise.

"The Lord gives and the Lord takes away," Angie said, fingering the blue beads of her rosary.

"Ah, but, my maid, look what ye can do for your own self," Hannah said, determined to turn the young woman's face toward living instead of dying.

Hannah took the stethoscope out of her bag and shoved it under the covers close by Angie's woolly nightgown to warm its cold celluloid disc. She blew out the flames that had burned throughout the night in the oil lamps, shutting off their sooty, fetid fumes, and lighted a fresh lamp. Opening a primitive chest of drawers she drew out a patch-work quilt worked in little squares from the fabric of earlier lives. One small patch caught her eye for it was a red velvet heart with the two sides of the heart meeting in a cross deep in the middle. It was somebody's symbol of hope and salvation. Hannah wrapped the quilt around Angie's shoulders and then she opened the window to let in a slice of cold, fresh air.

"Breathe it in, Angie now. Breathe it all in to the baby. It's something you can do, sure."

Hannah reached under the covers for the now-warmed stethoscope and anxiously pressed the flat end onto Angie's round belly. Surprisingly, the baby's heartbeat was steady and strong. She then put the earpieces into Angie's ears and watched the young woman's eyes grow bright with wonder. Angie looked like someone placed under a spell.

"Oh, he sounds just like a fairy drummer, sure, Hannie, he does, a little troll with his drum under water, look!"

But Angie had not long to enjoy the magic of the stethoscope and her baby's heartbeat for she was suddenly seized with a stronger pain that knotted her muscles into a tight, hot bowl. Angie reached under her pillow for her rosary and the little blue beads passed steadily through her thin fingers.

Feeling the chill wind of helplessness pass over her, Hannah closed the window and gazed at the horizon, hoping for a sign of Dr. John. She knew that only a forceps delivery could save Angie. Only the long forceps and a general anaesthetic. Now Hannah had to decide how long she dared let Angie wait for Dr. John before she had to be bundled into a coach box on a komatik for the 22-mile trek to the hospital at Barton's Bight. If the weather held, they could do it in four, five, maybe six hours.

Hannah picked up one end of the rosary and looked at the pretty blue beads. She rubbed their glassy roundness between her fingers and thought of the hours of prayer the little beads had felt. Then Hannah reached out and brushed Angie's thick, curly auburn hair back from her face.

"It must be nice to pray with beads," Hannah said shyly, touching the cross attached to the beads.

Angie looked at Hannah in disbelief, wondering how anyone could pray without a rosary. But when she saw that Hannah was serious, Angie said, "If you would accept it as a gift, look, I've a like to give you an extra rosary I have. 'Twas given to me by a priest visiting here from Quebec. If you open the top drawer, 'tis on the right."

Hannah drew the rosary out from among Angie's few items of neatly folded lingerie. Holding the dark-green beads up to the light, she let them slide through her fingers again and again, as though to get the feel of a string of prayers. Then she took Angie in her arms and shared her heartfelt thanks.

Stepping swiftly out to the kitchen, Hannah put the rosary in her bag and looked out of the window, hoping for some sign of the doctor. Anxious though she was, she painted in her mind a picture of his arrival, of her joy at feeling his comforting presence, the two of them working side by side to save Angie and her baby.

"Take hope, my child," Hannah said as she strode back into the bedroom. "Fear and hope can't live side by side, look. So let's take hope."

Just then Angie propped herself up on one elbow and seized Hannah's arm.

"Listen, my maid, someone's coming!"

Chapter Four

Hannah felt a rush of cold air sweep into the bedroom as John strode into the house, stamping snow from his seal-skin boots and setting his medical bag on the kitchen table. From where she stood by Angie's bed, Hannah observed the kitchen scene reflected in the large bedroom mirror. She watched the doctor peeling off his white parka to uncover a well-worn blue turtleneck sweater and whipcord trousers.

As much for Angie as anyone, Tom called out in a high excited voice. "I'll go feed all the dogs now, look, and be back the once. And thanks be ye've come, doctor. Thanks be."

"I could hardly have missed this call, Tom. People from six homes called out to me with the message," he said in the deep jovial voice that always made something quicken within Hannah. His voice reached deep within her, stirring her body and mind with sensations she felt only with him.

Hannah was drawn to John's voice the very first time she heard it some twenty years earlier when he was twenty-nine and she was only fourteen. She heard the sonorous voice before she actually saw the doctor for he was speaking to a nurse around a curve in the corridor.

That morning he was telling his operating-room nurse, "We'll get in and get out!" using the surgeon's shibboleth for making the incision with one bold stroke, deftly performing the operation and closing the wound as quickly as possible. The necessity to "get in and get out" expeditiously may have been prompted by the patient's having a respiratory problem.

Do certain voices affect certain ears in a special way? Are there donor voices for receptor ears? Does the voice carry music from the soul in the same way the eyes offer a glimpse of the inmost spirit? Occasionally John's voice led Hannah to hear only the sound and miss some of the meaning. And often, to her distraction, Hannah found his voice continued to vibrate somewhere deep within her long after he had finished speaking.

Whenever Hannah felt confounded by the power John's voice had over her, she recalled having read a novel in which a man fell in love with a woman's voice even before he saw her. He was mysteriously bewitched by the spell she innocently cast on him with the mellow sound of her voice.

In the early days of knowing John, Hannah used to listen for the sound of his voice coming closer down a corridor. But this morning in the Prynns' home, under the desperate circumstances, Hannah wondered at herself for still being distracted by the doctor's voice. She quickly took herself in hand and once again checked Angie's blood pressure and the baby's heartbeat.

She heard John speak to the two elderly midwives and in the mirror she could see them nod to him in unison and yet still sit transfixed. Then slowly they rose as one dark memorial to motherhood and nodded again to him. When he turned toward the bedroom, they slipped out to return to their own homes.

"We're really glad you've come, Dr. John," said Hannah. "It's a shy baby we have here." And then she told him about the course of Angie's labour.

Those who did not know John well might at first have found his bearing aloof, even imperious, for he had a way of mastering any situation with his powerful presence. He took charge without ever deposing or denying others their rightful task and place. In fact, he made people feel more significant than they had ever believed themselves to be. Hannah knew from having worked with him that he was no strutting operating-room hero. John himself knew, from his often humbling experiences along the coast, that there was no room for either vanity or pride in the practice of medicine. Nor was John afraid to show his vulnerability, to admit to his feelings, or to understand how others felt as well. He made Hannah feel she was an indispensable colleague.

Having scrubbed his hands, John drew on a pair of sterile rubber gloves and went in to examine Angie, who lay like a sculpted arc curving in pain under the covers. Hannah watched John as he looked into Angie's face and she noticed a melancholic mistiness around his eyes. Whatever was different about him this morning seemed due to a personal sadness of some sort.

"Doctor, dear, I wondered if ye'd ever get here," Angie said, smiling up at John and holding the blue beads of the rosary across her unborn baby.

While John examined Angie, Hannah studied his face with its broad, sweeping, flat planes of cheeks tanned the year round from the sun and the wind. Having been travelling for two days, a dark stubble of beard was beginning to grow in, casting a bluish shadow over his chin and upper lip. His eyes were a brilliant blue, sparkling as though they had their own private sun.

His dark hair was streaked with silver at the temples and it grew thicker at the sides than on the top. His high sweep of forehead was underlined by a pair of thick, dark brows. His nose was long and straight. Slightly flaring nostrils carried on out to deep lines curving like loving parentheses down to the corners of his mouth. It was a mouth that always seemed perched on the edge of a smile.

"Angie, do you mind if we give you something to make you sleep while we bring the baby down?" he asked. To Hannah he said, "I know you can manage the anaesthetic."

Just as Angie nodded her consent, she was gripped with pain and a primitive cry escaped her lips.

Was Angie's cry a voice from her soul begging to be recognized and freed? Were the woman's hours of teetering at what she feared might be the gates of a premature eternity also a break in the sky, offering a glimpse of the person she could one day become, if she ever survived?

Most of the women on the coast took their clues for living from what they had observed in their mothers, their aunts, their older sisters and whatever made sense to them at the time. In most homes the women dried their clothes separately from the men's. Yet it was not difficult to pick up the trail of womanhood since there were few of the modern conveniences enjoyed by their sisters in the South or on the mainland. The men, for their part, were knowingly quiet on the subject of women's tribulations. When they spoke on the matter among themselves, they nodded their heads, sending dark arcs of tobacco spit out of their mouths to land where they might while thanking God they did not have to endure the ups and downs of "women's reeraws."

As for the young, there was little to buffer them from the reality of poverty and illness. In the tiny coastal villages the angel of death made its appearance as regularly at the cradle as at the rocking chair. The young were never shielded from the faces of the dead. Despite their tender years, the children and adolescents often wore the wisdom of the ages in their fresh, unlined faces.

John pulled off his examining gloves, opened a package of sterile obstetrical forceps and re-scrubbed his hands before putting on a fresh set of gloves. Hannah, by this time, was pouring ether over a cloth-covered, sieve-like mask above Angie's face.

"Blow it away, Angie. Blow it away." And every time Angie blew the merciful gas away, she took in another deep breath of it until she slipped into a deep sleep.

With Angie's anaesthetic under control, Hannah's eyes wandered toward John's hands. They were the same hands that had so skilfully brought Daniel into the world, that had dressed Hannah's caesarean incision.

Hannah had known John for some twenty years, yet to her he was still "doctor" — Dr. Weatherton or Dr. John. It was part of the communal teaching of the coast to remember one's place with those whom Morna called "the gentles," people of a higher social status, especially those "from away," such as Dr. John. And so Hannah often ended up calling the doctor nothing at all, for she knew him too well to be comfortable calling him by his formal name but not well enough to call him John.

As she stood near him, she smelled the cold, fresh air still lingering about him. She also sensed his own personal alchemy: a mingling of antiseptics, ether, something soapy and clean, something mysterious and male.

Perhaps it was the enormous relief at having Dr. John's help for Angie that gave her mind a freedom to soar and glide. She felt a burst of energy rising within her, a tide of power that made her steady herself against the bed.

Hannah still had the ether mask over Angie's face when Tom came in and stood shyly at the door. He walked over to Angie and wrapped the rosary around her motionless fingers. Then Tom looked from Hannah to John. "I'll be next door if ye needs me."

Hannah continued to give the anaesthetic, watching intently as John gently rode the forceps in around the baby's head. In the mirror she saw a small dark head being drawn from its human cave.

"Oh, 'tis born with a sillyhow over itself," Hannah said cheerily as John drew the amniotic sac away from the baby's face. "'Tis good luck to be born with a sillyhow. They say a person'll never drown if he's had one on!''

But John did not reply to her comment.

"It's a boy," he said laconically. "Another little fisherman."

Something flared inside Hannah at the doctor's pronouncement.

"Is it for everyone to be a fisherman? Not the only work in the world, sure.''

Hannah's words pierced whatever numbness enveloped John that morning. He understood why his words irritated Hannah and he was sorry he had said them. He knew she was anxious to spare her son Daniel the ignominy of trying to take his place on the tossing ships and slippery fish stages.

John also knew Hannah possessed a flinty system of reasoning. She took no one's opinion as her own before examining it carefully. When she listened to her people echoing what they had heard from their parents, she often questioned their thinking. As a result, she frequently found herself alone with her opinions. And so it was that she took her solace in reading books, building on her hard-won high school education.

From the days when she had worked at the hospital in Barton's Bight, the staff were inspired to send their discarded books down to Hannah in the Cove. She was their unofficial custodian and offered the books to anyone who wished to read them. But in the end the books moved back and forth between Hannah and her young neighbour Will Speke who also came alive in the world of books.

It was always an exciting day when a carton of books arrived in the Cove. Sometimes they came by boat, sometimes by a passing dog team. Hannah and Will unpacked them, eagerly scanning the titles, the authors, and ready to be carried away to the realms of the imagination.

Sometimes a book bore the signature of John Weatherton,

and Hannah always ran her fingers over the letters, as though they might even speak as she touched them. She liked to come upon underlined sentences for they brought her into the company of an earlier reader. And always she read the books inscribed with John's name first; they ran the gamut from English mysteries to cryptic philosophy.

She took the baby from John and lowered him into a basin of warm water, crooning a song she made up as she went along. Then she dried him in a warm towel and massaged oil into his firm little body.

"He's got a back like a little goose," she said as she rolled him over and dressed him in his oven-warmed clothes, swaying back and forth with him cradled in her arms. Then she offered the baby up for John to hold.

John smiled at Hannah through the weariness that follows travel on the trail for two days and three nights. As he lent his great frame tenderly to the tiny life he had just saved, Hannah remembered the morning she first saw Daniel, the morning after the harrowing trip to hospital fourteen years earlier.

She had awakened from her anaesthetic to find Haim holding her hand. She felt the stumps where the two fingers were missing and heard his husky voice. "Hannie, we have a fine lad. Would ye like to call him Daniel?"

Hannah looked into Haim's weary, unshaven face, at his rheumy, bloodshot eyes. She nodded a slow, steady yes.

"'Twill be a fine name for a boy, Haim," Hannah said with a touch of resignation. "A fine name for calling him in to supper." And Haim took a tender leave of Hannah and the baby.

One hour later John came in with Daniel in his arms. Hannah propped herself on one elbow and discreetly put the baby to a swollen pink breast.

Pensively she rolled the rim of one of the baby's ears between thumb and finger, steeling herself to ask John a question she would rather not have to ask.

"Can you tell me something, Dr. John. Will he be. . ."

John stroked Daniel's head tenderly. He looked into Hannah's eyes with their sad, questing gaze.

"It's too soon to tell. We'll have to watch how he develops. But you were right to come to hospital. The placenta was down low and if you'd stayed home, neither you nor Daniel would have made it. Next baby, come to hospital a month earlier, just to make sure. Oh, and you still have your uterus. Thought you might be worried about that."

During her days in hospital, Hannah looked out of her window and each morning saw John come down the hill from his home to the hospital, down the steep incline at a boyish half-run. Often in the evenings she watched him climb back up the hill between two rows of evergreens, toward the amber glow of a lamp burning in one window.

Hannah learned, from one person and another who knew Dr. John and his wife Cynthia, that they had met at Barton's Bight when she was doing a year of volunteer teaching. They were married a year later at her South Carolina home amid the heavenly pink magnolias, their boughs like arms offering great masses of blossoms. Some three hundred of Cynthia's friends shared the day. Over the strains of Strauss rose the excited, trilling voices of the women solicitously asking Cynthia, "Dahling, are there savages up there? You're so brave! But won't you simply freeze to death?"

As it turned out, Cynthia did not spend her winters in the North. She left the coast each November when the ice began to form, when the coastal steamers made their last calls with the mail and winter supplies and the villages and hamlets braced themselves for yet another drubbing from wintry storms.

She would return to the coast in the late spring, when

the only remaining snow lay far away on the distant hills like white sauce on peaks of spicy brown pudding. She would come back lightly tanned and relaxed after her winter in the sunshine that bathed acres of rolling hills and gentle streams winding through the estate in South Carolina that she had inherited from her parents.

Hannah had seen Cynthia around the hospital, where she taught the children who were confined to beds, braces, casts – often because of tuberculosis. She was petite and elegant, never trading her city shoes with their slim heels for rubber-soled walkers. Her country cashmeres and corduroys in shades of mossy green, tan, rust and brown set off her long auburn hair and distinguished her from the other women, most of whom wore practical parkas and windproof pants.

Until she returned each spring, John lived with an aged housekeeper called Abigail. His was an aesthetic life: a blend of work relieved by reading and listening to the music he loved. During World War II he had spent two years with the U.S. Navy in the Pacific while Cynthia stayed in the South.

As soon as Angie was awake, John laid the baby in her arms. The little mother felt for her rosary and tucked it under the baby's blanket.

John and Hannah were drinking tea in the kitchen when Tom returned. His eyes darted from one to the other, silently asking for news.

"You've a fine son, Tom," John said, "and Angie's fine, too."

Tom smiled shyly. He kicked off his boots and hurried in to Angie. After the purgatory he had been through during the past two days, when he was not sure what was to happen to Angie, it made little difference to him whether he had a son or a daughter.

Every couple understood anyway that the women did

fifty per cent of the work. Maybe more. A woman was an economic necessity. She was often the driving force in the family. Not only did she keep the house, the children and the garden, but she also helped to "make" the fish: stacking, salting, turning them to "get the spirit of the sun into them," as Morna called it.

The women did just about everything but go out in the boats to catch the fish. And even then they often broke sleep at two or three in the morning to make breakfast for the men who had to move smartly to catch the fish while the waters were open. The women had an equality, especially if they had strong backs and sturdy spirits. They worked hard but never made their fatigue a man's guilt.

Tom came out of the bedroom, his face glowing with pride. "I wants ye to know, doctor, we've a like to Christian the baby after ye — John, sir, John. 'Tis a fine name." Then he turned toward Hannah. "If ye and doctor could bide for a while, we'd share with ye the groanin' cake the women have made for Angie."

"Sorry, I can't. Have to get back to the hospital. But I think John's a fine name too," John replied.

"I have to get back to my family," said Hannah. "Ma's not too well betimes."

John drank the last of his tea. "Hannah, I'm heading north, going right past the Cove. I can drop you off. Just have to have a word with Father Machovie and see two patients. We can leave just after noon. Get you to the Cove late afternoon. Might as well save another team going north."

It was close to one that afternoon when Hannah and John took the trail that led from Abel's Eye to Steadman's Cove. As John's team of dogs made the last turn that carried them out of the village, Hannah looked back and saw the two old midwives making their way to the Prynns' house, their arms filled with dishes of food.

Chapter Five

Hannah left Abel's Eye in high spirits that January afternoon. Another child had been brought safely into the world. Craving some exercise, she trotted alongside the komatik, her sealskin boots skimming lightly over the trail.

John ran beside Hannah and from time to time they caught sight of an indigenous bird. Sometimes it was John who called out, "Look, there's a redpoll!" Another time Hannah asked, "Did you see the winter bunting just then?"

They welcomed the fresh cold air after the closeting warmth of the Prynn home. Every time the team was about to head down a hill, Hannah and John jumped back on the komatik like children eager for the thrill of racing through the cold tunnel of frigid air, feeling the tiny darts of snow flying back in their faces from the feet of the dogs.

Some of John's old friendliness was coming back, peeking out from behind the curtain of concern hanging around his eyes. Hannah wanted to ask him what was troubling him, but instead she said, "It's a grand airsome day, isn't it?"

"It's a wonderful day for travelling," he replied. "We should be able to make it to Steadman's Cove by late afternoon, Hannah. If the dark's coming on or there's a storm up there, I may have to stay in the Cove for the night and head on up to the Bight early next morning."

"There's always a bed ready for anyone who needs it at our house," Hannah said with a warm smile and a toss of her head.

John ran ahead to keep the dogs under control. Then he scooped up a handful of snow and made a snowball, tossing it playfully back at Hannah. She fended it off, sending it into crumbs before it could hit her. She packed a loose snowball of her own and threw it back at John. But he was momentarily distracted by something on the trail and the snowball hit him on the back of the head. It fell apart down his neck and some of it landed in the hood of his parka lying loosely down his back.

Embarrassed, Hannah hurried to catch up to him. She brushed the snow from his hood and away from the reddening skin of his neck.

"Sorry to get you like that," she said apologetically.

John just laughed and shrugged his broad shoulders. "Ever think you'd like to pitch baseball?"

Hannah laughed, mimicking his body language. It was the kind of banter she imagined she would have enjoyed with an older brother. She ran harder now, trying to catch up with John and the dogs, climbing up to the top of a steep hill. At the peak they looked out over the spectacular beauty of the snowy panorama spreading out in the valley before them. It was a carpet of white, save for the dark areas etched with sombre families of evergreens.

"Wherever could you see such a scene?" John asked. It may have been the company of Hannah, or the exhilarating wintry vista below them, that piqued John's daring and fearlessness as they were about to descend the long, steep hill. He decided not to throw the drag chain under the runner to brake their speed, and they flew down the hill, Hannah hanging onto John as though riding pillion on a motorcycle.

Down in the valley he turned to Hannah. "How did you like that for a ride?"

"I thought my head was going to fly off," Hannah said, stuffing her long blonde hair back up under her woollen cap.

Their headiness was short-lived, however, for as they made their way to the other side of the valley, they felt the first stinging pellets of driven snow on their faces. They looked at each other and John nodded toward the western sky which looked as though it had just collected all the heavy, blue smoke of a battlefield.

"I don't like the looks of the weather up ahead. But maybe it's only a passing squall. What do you think, Hannah?" John asked with the deference that an outsider wisely grants to someone who has grown up in the North.

"It looks like a proper weather-breeder. But I'm for going on because it's as far back to Abel's Eye as it is to the Cove," Hannah said. "Even if we were to go back, we'd be in the same storm moving south. Somewhere between here and the Cove there's a tilt — a little hut — where we can shelter until the storm clears."

And so with growing concern about the worsening weather, John and Hannah pressed on into the storm.

John looked at Hannah's upturned profile scanning the sky. He studied her as she ran, observing that she was just as clean-limbed, swift and quick of turn as she had been the first time he laid eyes on her twenty years earlier, when she was a nurse's aide working at the hospital. He reckoned she must be thirty-four years old now but she had retained the finely sculpted features in her upturned glance. She had the straight, thin nose and rounded high forehead that John always associated with clear thinking and constancy. As he looked at her running against the background of the darkening sky, he pondered her mysterious quality of always being able to communicate everything she was as a woman even when she was silent.

John recalled the first time he began to come under Hannah's spell, to feel he was becoming part of a drama that he could not quite control. It gave him an odd feeling for he was accustomed to being in charge of his own life and often of the lives of those around him.

That earlier morning when Hannah was just a slip of a girl, he had come upon her standing alone, gazing out of a hospital window at a brilliant winter sun rising up over the harbour. He found as he gazed at her that morning she seemed to quiver before his eyes, much as heat waves tremble above a hot city pavement. To his surprise, he saw her in a soft diffusion of light, like a halo around her entire body, and wondered if he was losing his usual sharp professional focus with which he viewed almost everybody. The sensation was both comforting and confusing to him for he was in the custom of passing his thoughts through the analytical, filtering, logical half of his brain, the drawer-tidying half of the mind.

He wanted to ask her, that earlier morning, what she was thinking as she gazed at the sun sending its cool splintering splendour darting over the waves in the harbour. But then he reminded himself that he was a married man and that she was only a girl of fourteen, although she seemed to have a rare sensual maturity and the womanly wisdom of all time. At that moment Hannah, completely unaware that anyone was watching her, was recalling on memory's private reel the cinematic scenes of her recent visit to Montreal where she had pushed open a door to the dawn of her womanhood in the mushroom pink of Belle's Venusian bathroom.

John turned to leave, but something inexplicable held him to the spot. As he looked at Hannah he knew there was still some earthy root to be pulled up and studied. He wondered if he might be becoming a bit "bushed," a common phenomenon among doctors and nurses working in isolated frontier settlements. Did he need a sabbatical? Was he spending too much of his life away from the friends, the theatre, the symphonies, the laughter that were all once such a large part of his life before he came to Newfoundland? He knew in his own heart, and certainly Cynthia had told him often enough, that he lived under the tyranny of his logic and his muscles.

But as he tried to analyze the persistent allure of Hannah, he remembered once reading a book about past lives. Could he conceivably have known her in another life? He even wondered if he might be going crazy in a persistent and professionally acceptable way. Was he sacrificing his life on the altar of medicine and all of its demands? If so, he rationalized, might he be justified in savouring Hannah's sensuousness to the fullest possible delights?

Just at that precise moment, Hannah turned her head slightly in a certain, familiar way. John knew in one iridescent flash the solution to his dilemma. He saw, to his utter amazement, that Hannah looked stunningly like a younger version of his first fiancée, a tall, blonde and beautiful Swedish woman called Karina who, just before they were to be married, was killed in a car accident.

In his moment of realization, John felt both older and younger than his twenty-nine years. He was not, after all, inclined to reach in and rob from the cradle. Quietly he turned and walked away down the empty corridor with his thoughts about Hannah continuing to haunt him.

In the years after that mystical experience, each of John's meetings with Hannah etched her being and soul deeper and deeper into his mind. They were often — almost fatefully — thrown together and frequently in times of tension in the hospital. Because of Hannah's eagerness to learn and her superior intelligence, John taught her how to give anaesthetics, a role she often fulfilled while he excised a piece of tissue that had become an insult to someone's body.

As he looked at Hannah trotting into the gathering storm with him on their way to Steadman's Cove, he recalled one particular evening many years earlier when they were brought together in their work. It was just one year before Hannah was to meet and marry Haim. On this evening John was about to go home and was passing the single room isolated at the end of the ward and reserved for the critically ill. His own blend of caring and curiosity caused him to push open the door and look in.

In the subdued light of the depressing room he saw Hannah holding a dying man in her arms. She was easing his last shuddering breaths by humming something John recognized as Mozart's exquisitely beautiful *Eine Kleine Nachtmusik*. He slipped into the room and stood silently beside her in the indigo shadows spreading out from the dark-blue paper she had wrapped around the bedside lamp to soften its glare.

John stayed with Hannah through the man's dying hour and together they shared the final tasks the living offer the dead. Their work finished, John moved the chairs back to the wall. It was then he saw a book lying on the floor, a book Hannah had obviously been reading. He picked it up, recognizing the familiar, claret-coloured leatherbound volume of Palgrave's *Golden Treasury of Poetry*.

He opened it up and saw his own writing, affectionately inscribing the book to Cynthia on the occasion of her birthday the year before they were married. John nostalgically remembered having ordered the book by mail from New York. He felt a moment of melancholy as he realized that his earlier gift, so tenderly proferred to Cynthia, had found its way from their bookshelves to the bales of books that were sent to the people in the villages along the coast.

John loved poetry and as he let the pages fan open, a poem flashed through his mind. Was it Edna St. Vincent Millay who wrote about the pain of a dying love? He tried to remember what the poet had written about an un-armoured heart feeling the pangs of a love whose embers were growing cold. *It was not love's going that hurt my days. . .just that it went. . .in little ways. . . .*

The moment Hannah saw John open the book and read his own writing in the inscription, she was filled with empathy for him as she sensed his acute embarrassment. He handed the book to Hannah and kissed her softly on one cheek. She was then eighteen years old and becoming progressively more beautiful.

"I'm glad you're enjoying this anthology," he said, recovering himself.

"I love poetry," Hannah replied, riffling through the thin, silky pages of the book. As she turned her face up to him and smiled, John was struck more forcibly than ever by her striking similarity to his long-deceased fiancée.

As they continued their dog-team trip, John gazed at Hannah against winter's indigo sky and realized that now, twenty years after he had first seen her, she was just as much of an enigma, still a delightfully unexplained mystery. As the snow flung itself in his face, he was aware that he never looked at her without wanting to share all of her world — her thoughts, her feelings, her hopes for her life. In the same vein he wanted her to know everything about himself: what he was like as a boy growing up in Maine, how he learned to sail a boat, how he liked to sit before a hearth at night and hear a log roll over on itself.

What power did she possess, he wondered, to make him feel that he could run up to the moon and back? What magic did she work that he now overlooked the shortness of his breath? What alchemy did she possess that gave him easy access to memories of old stairways from his childhood, a creaking hinge, a postman's smile — as well as easy entry to a world of wisdom, information that he hardly knew was his? Why, in her fair company, did he forget the spectre of those long winter months when Cynthia was in the sunny South watching one cliff swallow after another touch and skim the lovely lake that lay beyond the lawns of her estate?

John jumped off the komatik and ran beside the dogs to keep them pulling steadily through the blinding blizzard, through sheets of snow curtaining the trail before them. But the dogs were still willing to struggle on and Hannah had to run faster through the deepening snow to keep up with John and the team.

When Hannah caught up with John, they looked into each other's faces and laughed for they were each other's mirror reflecting their faces with brows and lashes whitened to instant agedness with the heavy snow. They brushed the hoary snows of age from each other's face, laughing at an easy distance from time's warp, although John felt the curve of time more pointedly than Hannah. They smiled again, aware that their breaths rose like two small clouds drifting together, only to be buffeted and scattered by the restless wind.

John was concerned about how much farther they had to go to reach the tilt, but he trusted Hannah's judgement. He knew something of her legendary solo trip out into a wintry night, driving a team of dogs when there was no one else to take her down the coast to help an old man who had a fish bone stuck in his throat.

The outport women did not often drive dog teams any more than they went out in the boats with the men. But that night Hannah had managed to reach her patient and remove the bone lodged like a sword in his throat. On her return, she was caught in a storm which she survived only by spending the night in a tilt.

The tilts were simple wooden huts scattered here and there along the dog-team trails. They were often built on a site where someone had perished in a storm or come perilously close to it. Often there was a blanket or two, a package of tea, a box of biscuits, a tin of soup, all left in gratitude by a previous survivor. It was understood that each beneficiary would leave a bundle of firewood and food enough for the next victim of winter.

Hannah watched John send the whip ripping out above the dogs. She thought of Haim and the many times she had seen him dexterously fling his whip out and bring it back to coil like a snake at the front of the komatik. Hannah tried to fight her fatigue by thinking of home and the warmth of her family.

To an outsider Hannah's family might have seemed like a sorely afflicted lot. But Haim did not sit around mourning either his missing fingers or his ribs. And Morna, although crippled, was held in great respect, as were all the elderly and infirm along the coast. She still held the household in her matronly thrall. And Daniel, who might have seemed the most beleaguered of all, held his head high with a quiet dignity and a sense of his own true worth. Hannah's family, like most of the people in Steadman's Cove, gave little thought to what they did not have. They looked not to the withered leaves of autumn but to the sticky, swelling buds of spring.

Hannah, bowing her head to escape the stinging pellets of snow flying into her face, took comfort that her family would be spared any concern for her well-being on this stormy night for they would assume she was still safely sheltered at the Prynns.

Now the dogs were straining through the snow and John and Hannah once again jumped off the komatik to ease the burden of their heavy haul. After a while John saw that Hannah was beginning to fall behind and he dropped back to run beside her, to share her struggle through the snow. Again they smiled at each other, for this time, with their pointed hoods encased in a glaze of ice and snow, they looked like monks from the Middle Ages, or maybe prisoners treading out their last few measured steps to the gruesome, gaping guillotine.

"Why don't you ride for a while, Hannah?" John said. "It's pretty level here now. Just hop on."

Hannah climbed onto the komatik again, easing the steady aching in her legs, until they came to yet another hill when she jumped off and ran behind John. But the moment they reached the top, Hannah dropped onto the sled again. Beginning to feel drowsy, she stirred herself on for she knew about the ominous sleepiness preceding death by freezing, a fate that had claimed many a winter traveller just a few hundred yards from shelter. Hannah took in long deep breaths of the air warmed by the scarf now wrapped around her face.

It was just at this point she was almost certain she saw the tilt a few hundred yards ahead, a little to the left of the trail. Was it not the same tilt she had stayed in, its grey form blanketed under a snowy roof?

Once again Hannah jumped off the komatik and ran until she caught John by the arm. Breathlessly she said, "I think I saw the tilt — just up there ahead on the left."

John kept on running, scanning the direction in which Hannah pointed. He peered intently into the storm and shook his head. "I can't see any tilt, Hannah. Where was it you saw it?"

Hannah pointed to where she was sure she had seen the little grey hut. But now, to her confusion, she saw nothing except more blinding snow.

"Funny thing. I can't see it myself just now. But I know it's up there. Just ahead on the left. And I know it was not a mirage!"

Hannah had read how weary travellers on deserts of sand or snow might see mirages, phenomena lacking in any ultimate substance. But she also understood how, when pushed to the limits of human survival, more than one pioneer staggering through the sand or the snow had had a fleeting intuition, a vision beyond any conscious view of reality. It was a kind of superior intelligence that took over where logic left off. Was such a pre-vision granted travellers to keep them from giving up and perishing on the trail?

As the storm raged on, Hannah struggled to keep going, though she was purblind from the tiny stinging stones of snow that seemed to lash the more cruelly as the two of them grew ever wearier staggering on through the dusk. Her legs felt like loose, spent elastic, and she longed to lie down in the snow and sleep.

John, who now watched Hannah's pace ever more closely, called back to her, "Keep on going, Hannah! Keep going! We're almost there!"

She struggled and staggered on again. She watched John reeling from time to time. She saw him fall and feared he might be having a heart attack.

Hannah ran to John and held out her hands to help him up to his feet. Now the pressure to keep up with the dogs had eased off a little for they were caught up in a fight that did not, for the moment at least, involve the lead dog. John staggered up and together they untangled the dogs.

John looked into Hannah's face with concern. "You'd better sit on the box, Hannah. You look really exhausted. I'm sure it's not very far now."

There was no sign of relief from the storm and no sign of the tilt either. When the dogs started to founder again, Hannah jumped off and ran for a while. In her weak and weary state she had no idea how much later it was when John took her by the arm and shouted, "Look, Hannah, there's the tilt! Up there on the left. You were right! Can you go on up by yourself while I tie up the dogs?"

Hannah nodded and struggled on toward the tilt.

"Keep on going, Hannah," she heard John shout when she was not even aware she had stopped. "Keep going! You're almost there."

Hannah reached for the handle of the tilt and tried to

open the door, but it was frozen fast. She threw herself against the door again and again, like a frenzied animal launched into perpetual motion. Then suddenly the door gave way and Hannah flumped through its dark open space to fall full length on the wooden floor.

Lying motionless where she had fallen in the dark of the windowless hut, Hannah closed her eyes against the cold and her terrible exhaustion. When she heard John's boots sliding across the floor, she opened her eyes and looked up into his face. He slipped one hand under her head to cushion it and she felt his warm breath on her cheek.

"Hannah, Hannah!" he said softly. "You did it!"

"We did it," Hannah said as she reached into her pocket for a tissue to wipe away a drip trembling at the end of John's nose. Then she touched his mottled cheeks. "You've got a bit of frostbite here and there."

A look of love crept around John's eyes. It had been some time since he had felt a woman's caring. He smiled and with his bare hand brushed the snow from Hannah's hair. Then he helped her up to her feet while their eyes grew accustomed to the dark and took stock of the hut.

"I know where there's a lamp and some matches," Hannah said, recalling her previous experience.

"And I know where there's some wood — waiting to be cut," John replied with a laugh. "I'll go now and bring in a supply for the night."

Before closing the door behind him, John paused to look at Hannah lighting the lamp, filling the grim, grey shelter with a warm glow and lending her face the softness of a child's on Christmas Eve.

Chapter Six

In the middle of the room stood an old black stove with a sooty-bottomed aluminum kettle on top. A spindly stove-pipe rose up to penetrate a hole through the roof of the tilt. In one corner, along with a heap of firewood, lay a stack of old newspapers — one headline predicting that union with Canada would be "closely contended." On one end of a surrogate bed — a board braced to the wall — lay a pile of grey blankets and a meagre supply of tinned food.

John soon returned with the wood and Hannah shut the door behind him against the drifting snow. But the door that only moments earlier was frozen shut now would not stay closed.

"I'll jam it shut with a split of wood," John said, and together they secured the door, their wooden shield against the night's bitter cold and driving snow. "It's such a relief to be able to speak without having the wind blow your words back into your mouth."

Hannah shivered from a combination of the cold, the relief of being safe, her exhaustion, and maybe at the thought of being alone in the tilt with John.

"You're cold, Hannah, dear," John said tenderly as he wrapped a blanket about her shoulders and set to rolling up newspapers, laying splits of wood in the stove's dark belly and setting it on fire. "We'll warm this place up in no time at all."

"I'm fine now," Hannah said with a little laugh. "'Twas just the storm, oh, and the worry of Angie."

"You were in a tight spot, Hannah. No question about that," John said, sliding back the stove lid to let the fire draw better. Soon the hut was filled with the sound of the flames scuttering up the chimney like racing dogs taking off on a dirt track.

"I kept putting from my mind my own terrible dog-team trip to the Bight the night Daniel was born. I had to keep sending the memory away and replacing it with pictures of Angie's baby being born pink and sweet, with you and me delivering the little one. And you were there to save us both," said Hannah.

As they warmed themselves at the stove, happy to be out of the wind whistling around the corners of the tilt, a gentle awkwardness crept in around them. Hannah and John had spent many hours working together in the hospital and out in the villages, but it was always in the company of others.

Hannah stared into the shadowy, unlighted corners of the tilt. There crept into her memory lines from a poem about the dusk and the daylight. She turned her eyes to John's chiselled profile jutting out from under his woollen cap.

"Did you ever learn a poem about the children's hour — about a pause in the day when the light was beginning to lower? Somehow this place with its shadowy corners reminds me of it."

John looked into Hannah's eyes and with a smile that softened his whole face, he entered into her mood and began to feel younger than his forty-nine years.

"There was Alice and laughing Allegra and Edith with golden hair," he said softly, recalling a poem he had not thought of since he was a child.

"They were the blue-eyed banditti!" Hannah replied.

Lowering his voice to the mock menacing tone of the villain, John said, " 'I have you fast in my fortress and will not let you depart, but put you down into the dungeon in the round-tower of my heart.' "

Hannah smiled tenderly at John, delighted that he shared her pleasure in the poem. Then, drawn to look up at the wooden roof, she playfully shadow-boxed John's head with hers and he merrily bunted hers back. But the sudden explosion of a bit of resin in the stove made Hannah stiffen as though she had just heard a warning shot from Haim. Guessing Hannah's thoughts, John wanted to take her in his arms and hold her close, for she quickened everything he had ever known of himself as a man.

Hannah saw that John's face had lost the sadness of the morning, when his eyes were hung with the dry, cast-off crusts of disappointment. But one hungering seemed to have been replaced with another.

John looked down into Hannah's face. Then with one finger he slowly and gently traced around her mouth, silently laying a seal upon their love.

"I'm going back out to settle the dogs for the night and bring in the box."

Hannah reached for the kettle as John made his way to the door, heading out into the night. He bucked against the wind, while Hannah stooped down and filled the kettle with snow at the side of the door.

John was soon back with the medical box from the komatik and together they hoisted it through the door and up beside the stove. Then he went back out into the night to cut more wood, leaving Hannah to delve into its depths for dishes and food. As she lifted the lid, there came the familiar smells of ether, oil of cloves, carbolic acid and Friar's balsam mingled with the scorched odour of cloth wrapped around surgical instruments baked to sterility in the hospital's autoclave.

While rummaging through the box for food, Hannah came upon three of John's books. She drew them out to the lamplight. One, she saw, was *Steppenwolf* by Hesse. Another was a well-worn book by a surgeon who had accompanied Captain Cook on his South Sea journeys to the Antipodes. The third was *The Deerslayer* by James Fenimore Cooper. Hannah flicked through the pages, some of them underlined, imagining John reading the books by lamplight in whichever fisherman's home he might be spending the night while out on a call.

Down at the bottom of the box Hannah found a tin of biscuits, some cheese, tinned meat, Carnation milk and a can of clam chowder. She put the chowder on to heat and laid out the rest of the supper on the bunk. Then turning over the biscuit tin to use its shiny under-surface as a mirror, Hannah combed her long, blonde hair up on top of her head, tucking it in with combs and pins.

She was writing about the day's dramatic events in her diary when John came back in.

"What's that you're writing?"

"It's my diary. I write in it every night. The people in the Cove see more drama than most people do in a large city. We feel whatever a neighbour is feeling."

"You're certainly right about the drama up here in the North," John agreed. "Sometimes I think I live two days in every one!"

Hannah looked up at him from her diary and smiled, giving him the little Newfoundland nod the outporter reserves for a mainlander.

"Now let me see," she said, feigning deep thought, "that would make you nigh onto one hundred years old, Dr. John!"

She stood up to stir the chowder. Her thoughts turned to home, to her good neighbour Emma Speke, who would have likely taken a dish of something over for supper this evening and helped her mother out of at least a few layers of flannelette for the night. Morna's chamber pot, Hannah suspected, would probably await her return.

"Mm, when I smell that chowder I know I'm starving," John said, taking in a deep breath of the appetizing aroma. "But I'm going out for another load of wood. Even with the stove giving its all, the place is still not very warm."

John was gone longer than he had the first time, and Hannah tied up the hood of her parka and went out into the night. She stood for a moment, listening for the cry of anyone who might be lost in the stormy night. Then she hurried toward the woods, her feet sinking deeply into the fresh, soft snow.

John saw Hannah before she spotted him because his eyes were more accommodated to the dark.

"Whatever are you doing out here?" he called, the wind catching his breath.

"I just came out to see if you needed any help." Then Hannah reached up to take part of his load and together they trudged back to the tilt.

"Somewhere in here there's a bottle of whiskey," said John, rummaging through the box. "It'll warm us up a bit tonight."

"It's down to the left. I saw it in there," Hannah said, serving the clam chowder. Then she shook out the blankets, folded them and spread them on the floor.

John mixed them each a drink, using some distilled water he had found in the box. Then he sank down onto the blankets, resting his back against the bench, while Hannah sat across from him leaning against the box.

"Well, here's to us," John said. "I think we did really well to get through that storm."

"I'll drink to that," Hannah said warmly. After the first sip she added, "And now let's drink to the newest New-foundlander. Here's to Master John Prynn. May he master his ship of life well!" And they clinked their tin mugs.

John raised his cup again. "Here's to your having a vision of this tilt long before it was visible."

"It was real enough to me," Hannah said lightly. "Real enough up here on the edge of the ocean."

"You know, Hannah, I was just thinking as I carried in the wood that if the world were a head, you might say we're sitting up here on the tip of one of its ears."

Hannah laughed and as she passed John his chowder, she said, "That reminds me of the tall tales a teacher used to tell us about this part of the world. Tales the discoverers used to take back to the Old World. How cod were so thick you could hardly get a rowboat through them. How there were one-legged creatures running up and down the shores. Unipeds, the teacher called them. Oh, and the sheep all had red wool. Can you imagine anyone ever believing such nonsense?"

"Well, you see," John said, "the New World was going to provide everything — spices, precious stones, silks — all part of the Renaissance dream. The Old World liked to call it idealism. But there was greed among their fantasies too. I once read how even Cabot's barber planned to have an island or two for himself."

Hannah wanted to hear John's views on confederation with Canada, but before she asked, he turned the conversation around.

"So you spent a night alone in this tilt. I thought women didn't drive dog teams up here!"

"When that message came over the news that I was needed in Horton's Harbour to take the fish bone out of Jake Brent's throat, I had to go. But the men were either away in the woods tending their traplines or sick with a terrible flu. Even Haim was sick — and determined I wasn't going alone. It was fine going down, but coming home I was caught in a storm. Struggled on as far as this tilt. Then I found there wasn't enough wood to last the night."

John leaned forward attentively. "I've heard various versions of this adventure. Now I'm glad to hear it straight from you, Hannah."

"Well, I took in the littlest husky from the dog team to keep me warm. We wrapped up in a blanket, maybe the one that you're on," Hannah teased, "and hunkered down until it was light enough to go on."

John knew that no one in the North ever tried to make a pet of a sled dog since they were often part wolf and untamed.

"Why did you take that chance," John asked, "when you knew how fierce they can be?"

"I knew the risk I was taking in crossing the border between driver and dog. But I trusted this little fellow and he trusted me. He was the runt of the litter. Haim wanted to get rid of him right after he was born. 'A small dog's a curse to himself and his driver. The big dogs just give him a miserable time.' But I persuaded Haim to let the little fellow live. Sometimes I had to smuggle him into the house to care for him when he was sick."

"You just don't seem the type to huddle down with a dog. Weren't you afraid he'd turn on you?" John asked, swirling his chowder around in his cup.

"It was very simple. I'd gone out to help a man and now I had to help myself. And that dog was as biddy as a lamb. It was as though he remembered the warm milk and bread I gave him when he was sick. Oh, sure, he smelled. And I can still see his taggety ears torn in the dog fights. But dawn came and we soon reached home. Just in time for breakfast with Haim: cold shoulder and hot tongue!

"Haim's not a man to get angry often, but that morning he banged his fist on the table, sending a spurt of tea up into the air. He shook his spoon at me. 'That was very dare of you, woman. Have you gone a bit seeney-sawney, taking off with the dogs? Have you never heard of dogs eatin' a person alive? Well, a team once et a man — not very far from here!'

"But Ma understood. She told Haim, 'Hannah was dutified to go. She cast her bread on the waters for that pup and he came through with the warmth for her. Ye can't go wrong by doin' what's right, Haim Holt!' "

John understood that Haim and Hannah loved each other in their own way. He was also aware that they lived in a part of the world where survival was a struggle and where there was little room for the kind of romantic love that is the privileged preserve of a small segment of western society, a society where a woman may be elevated to a lofty pedestal up out of the way, with little room to turn around. Any move she takes toward her freedom imperils her at such a height as well as those who are too near her heel or her toe.

As John tried to understand how Hannah's life and marriage moved, he thought perhaps Haim, in his anxiety for Hannah's safety, tried to restrain her too much, thus making her even more daring. But John surmised daring had been ingrained in Hannah from conception.

The wind was still whistling around the corners of the tilt and although the fire was drawing well, it was too cold for them to take off their outdoor clothing. John lay sprawled out on the blanket, relaxed; but Hannah noticed the wistful pain around his eyes and she wanted to ask him how life was with him.

She felt his eyes studying her and saw that he now had a quizzical look, as though a diagnosis he were seeking continued to elude him. Hannah could not contain her curiosity.

"What's on your mind when you have that look on your face?" she asked.

"If you really want to know, Hannah Holt, you remind me of someone. I might as well tell you. You remind me of a beautiful Swedish woman called Karina I once loved. In fact, we were engaged to be married when she was killed in a car accident.''

For a while they sat in silence. Hannah held John's hand tenderly in hers for she knew he had shared something poignant and deep in his heart.

Chapter Seven

That night in the tilt Hannah wanted John to know everything about her life, her family. Gently she began, "My
father was a man from away. From Sweden actually. A sea
captain who put into the Cove during a storm. Ma was just
a young widow."

John turned attentively to Hannah in her moment of
sharing. "How did you find out who your father was?"

"From my sister Belle. Once when I was visiting with
her and her husband in Montreal, she told me. And I wanted
to know too. Ma would never answer my question completely. She'd only say, 'Oh, he were jest a man from away,
Hannie.'"

Hannah held out her hands in a gesture of honesty and
shrugged her shoulders. Leaning toward John, she said,
"But you know, John, I can understand why Ma clammed
up and wouldn't talk about my father. She loved the man.
And that made all the difference to me. Up here nobody
worries about who your pa is. What matters is what kind
of person you are."

Looking at John with a merry twinkle, Hannah said,
"Of course it was an enormous relief to stop wondering if
my pa might be someone around the corner in the Cove.
And the more Ma kept it from me, the more certain I
thought it might be someone from the Cove. Oh, and what

a relief it was to know the truth. It set me freer than I ever dreamed I could be." And Hannah's carefree laughter filled the hut.

In that moment it was all John could do to restrain himself from taking Hannah in his arms, holding her clear laughter while it still bubbled up within her.

"Of course," he said reassuringly, "it's looked on very differently up here on the coast. You're accepted for the person you are, rather than for who your parents happen to be."

"Well sure, I'm a merry begot," Hannah said with a shrug as she peeled off her outer jacket and tossed it aside. "But at least I know I was begotten in love. I suppose I'm a love child. And do you know, John, I'm certain that Ma still loves the man who fathered me."

Hannah's face became soft and thoughtful. "I sometimes think my differentness, my likeness to my true father, may just be a sad reminder to Ma, and I can understand that. There are days when I'd like to see my father, to know what he's really like, and where he is now. I sometimes look out over the ocean and wonder if he still sails on the high seas."

As John gazed fondly at Hannah sitting across from him in her heavy sweater and outdoor slacks, he imagined what she would look like wearing a pretty dress, stockings, high-heeled shoes. He remembered sadly that he once knew Cynthia's measurements by heart. He wondered what size Hannah wore. What colours would she wear best? Deep blue? Dark coral as a backdrop against her fair hair?

He fantasized that if they lived in a city or town he would send her flowers in the morning, maybe yellow roses and daisies or blue and red anemones. Perhaps he would also, like the courtly, ancient Japanese, send her a gracious "pillow note," some little lines of love to be delivered by the earliest possible courier.

John stood up and stretched his muscles now stiff and

sore from the trip. He felt restless but alive in a way he had not known for years. Leaning down, he put his hands lightly on Hannah's shoulders and his smile caressed her face.

"Thank you, dear Hannah, for sharing your story with me." And he knelt down and took her in his arms. The wind brattled at the timbers of the hut and he felt Hannah stir as though she had been reminded of home and Haim. Sensing her dilemma, he released his embrace. In that moment John knew more fully than ever just how lonely he had felt being married to Cynthia.

John grew restless and unsettled. He wondered how Hannah contained her feelings for he sensed she was a passionate woman. He poured them each another drink and Hannah set out some biscuits and cheese.

"Let's pretend we're at a party," she said, "mingling with friends. So let's trade places. I'll lean on the bunk. You try your back against the box. And now here's to union with Canada. I'm all for it — from what I can tell," Hannah said with a lilt in her voice. She leaned back against the bunk. "How do you feel about the chance of confederation with the mainland — and what do you think it would be like for us?"

"I'm no prophet," John said. "But it'll surely mean a higher standard of living for everyone. There'll be roads joining all the outports, cars and motorbikes. The dog team will be replaced by a kind of snowmobile."

"I expect it'll be a mixture of both bane and blessing. But it has to be better than the deal the fishermen have now, with the fish merchants just giving them enough to starve on."

"There'll be change at all levels, for sure, Hannah. Dancing will change from the jigs and reels to whatever's popular in the States and Canada. Probably some kind of jive. But one good thing will be the roads. Easy for patients to go back and forth from hospital. There'll be more money around too. And one day Newfoundland may discover it has riches of its own. It may find an economic independence. What do you think about it, Hannah?"

"I had an interesting experience last spring," she said, "when I flew from Slipper Inlet back to Steadman's Cove in a politician's plane. Just a few days earlier Haim had taken me down to the Inlet by dog team to stay with a little girl who had pneumonia. But when it was time for me to go home, there was a mild spell — too little snow for dogs, too much ice for a boat. Then one morning we heard the droning of a bush pilot's seaplane passing overhead. It circled and dropped down on a pond just behind the Inlet. Suddenly we could hear the distant strains of a wavering voice on a record player singing 'The Wearing of the Green.' The plane settled down and onto the pontoon stepped a natty politician from the South, speaking for confederation. Black suit, bear-greased hair and all. The plane couldn't come in any closer than thirty feet from the shore because of the rocks in the shallow water."

"And what was he promising to do for you?" John asked.

"Well, for one thing, he promised there'd be jobs in the factories for every man-jack of them, yes, and with the finest kind of wages. 'You'll be able to burn a lot of your smelly old boats,' said he, 'and move from these little out-ports to join others in larger communities.'

"When he'd finished his spiel, I shouted that I was a midwife and if he was going up north would he take me as far as Steadman's Cove. Well, I've not had much practice at swimming, but I waded across, holding the medical bag above my head. It wasn't so deep, but was it ever cold! Oh, and you should have heard the folks on the shore shout and whistle as I clambered onto one pontoon and then into the plane — wetter'n a whale!"

John leaned back against the box, his legs stretched out, his head resting against his clasped hands, the way men will. He beamed proudly at Hannah.

"I bet you surprised him!"

"Perhaps, but I was really embarrassed about the puddle my wet clothes made, dripping all over the floor of the plane. But it didn't seem to bother the politician, who kept right on talking, talking, talking.

" 'Look,' he said, 'just look down there at this island of Newfoundland. It's mine. All mine!'

" 'Sir,' I said, 'it's the island of a people — our people, yours and mine — who gave it its spirit, who made it live in spite of the merchants in the South. It's their island. Nobody else's. And it never will be!' "

"Good for you, Hannah," said John, pounding a fist on the floor. "And what did he say to that?"

"It made little impression on him. But it bothered me to think of the coastal people being moved here and there, jammed this way and that, like a herd of caribou. Now I have to consider whether we might all move out to Montreal. My brother-in-law, Belle's husband, says he could get work for Haim in his shipping company, but Haim says he'll die with his rubber boots on his feet. And I know Ma'll never go. But if the way is clear this fall, maybe Daniel and I'll go out to see how he gets along away from the coast. John, he's a wonderful boy, and I want him to have his chance to be the best of himself."

John sighed and shook his head thoughtfully. He unzipped his outer jacket.

"And what about you, Hannah? What's best for you?"

"Oh, I'll manage, John. I've always managed somehow," she said. With a smile and a knowing glance, she excused herself and stepped out into the cold night to answer nature's call.

Standing for a moment outside the tilt, Hannah breathed in the sharp, cold air, contemplating the awesome calm that often followed a winter storm.

In the meantime, back in the tilt John nibbled a cracker and reflected on what Hannah had told him. He thought how often the women of the coast just seemed to accept what came their way as their inevitable lot in life. Were the lives of the outport women just the extreme of the frustrations in women's lives everywhere? he wondered.

As he stood up and fastened his coat to go outside and follow Hannah's example, he thought that perhaps the outporters' dignified acceptance of their lot was probably their true wisdom after all — for generations of fisherfolk.

Outside in the night the world was a crystalline cathedral of breathtaking beauty with the snow reflecting the light from a pale, misty full moon overhead. John looked at his watch and could hardly believe it was half-past two. He had never known time to fly so quickly.

He turned to see Hannah running around from the back of the tilt with the breathless air of excitement John loved about her. In the past twelve hours her enthusiasm had stirred him to feeling alive again and he realized she had a subtle way of peeling back the edges of the clinical mask he often wore to protect himself but which could also close him off from the give-and-take of loving feelings.

Reaching up to one corner of the tilt, Hannah snapped off an icicle and wrote John's name in the snow. Holding up the icicle, she smiled and said, "When I was little, we used to call this an ice candle."

John took the icicle and wrote Hannah's name in the snow. Then looking at the name, he said, "I've just noticed that your name spells the same forward as backward. That's supposed to be lucky."

"I've always been lucky," Hannah said. "I remember the first day I noticed that my name was a palindrome — though I didn't know the name for it then. But I ran to Ma, waving a little piece of paper to share my discovery. Ma just looked me in the eye and said, 'See to it, Hannah, that you're the same yourself — the same coming as going.'" And Hannah brushed one mitten against the other.

"That you are, Hannah," John said. "You surely are."

Looking up into the night, Hannah pointed to the sky. "Would you look at that moon. You'd think it was holding a drifty veil over its face. Gives everything a strange, soft look."

They stood silently enjoying the panorama of Northern Lights playing across the dome of the sky, one colour giving way to another like a drift of dancers swaying in a harem, their dresses of palest green, pink and lavender shifting as though they were being blown by the warm sirocco of a sultan's breath.

As they gazed at the heavens, Hannah and John both knew that they were observing the beginning of a new curve of time in the circle of life.

Chapter Eight

Back in the tilt they stoked the fire and settled in for the night. For a few moments John looked numbly off into one corner. Hannah knew that to ask what was troubling him would be to intrude on his privacy.

He sat down on the medical box, his elbows resting on his knees. Then he looked up at Hannah with a wistful smile. "Cynthia sent me a telegram this week. It came just before I left the Bight. She's not coming back this summer. She's staying in the South for good now."

By the time he returned home, the whole of Barton's Bight would know the contents of the telegram. A telegram sent to the North was just about as private as a message broadcast over the evening news. Sadie Black, Twyla Henson's sister, was the postmistress and telegraph operator at the Bight; and when it came to spreading news, especially personal gossip, one sister was as good at it as the other.

Hannah looked at John's tension-filled face. She was not used to seeing his jaw muscles clamp and writhe beneath the skin and it made her feel ill at ease. John leaned back and stared absently into space.

"She may change her mind and come back, John," Hannah said, at the same time wondering what John honestly felt. Did he perhaps feel more a sense of anger than loss? Had his marriage ever been ideal? Hannah looked at his jaw set against feeling his pain and she thought that even when he was frustrated and foiled, he still had the most interesting face she had ever seen.

"Usually when Cynthia makes up her mind about something, Hannah, that's it. But I'm hoping to go out to the States for a while this fall if I can find a *locum tenens* to fill in for me. Then I'll find out what's going on with my absentee wife. She may, of course, have found herself a southern lover, a gentleman of leisure who's always there on time for dinner and who doesn't have to cope with the problems of the sick," John said, his handsome features set in cynicism.

In the silence of the tilt Hannah tried to understand why John's sadness always crept over him like an untimely dusk just after they had laughed together, sharing some small joke. Did the centres for laughter and sadness live side by side in the mind? Or was it that their pleasure together in small, silly things — like writing their names in the snow — reminded John of happiness he had missed in his marriage, of laughter not laughed, of happiness that had always seemed halved and never quite whole?

Now there was only the sound of the flames in the stove sputtering cheerily up into the night as Hannah and John sat side by side. She longed to draw his head down into her lap, that comforting curve that seems to be more a part of a woman's landscape than a man's.

Marriage on the coast often grew naturally out of a friendship that had its roots in childhood. It was taken for granted that couples "walking out" would eventually marry. They understood that the mystical union to which they had plighted their troth was forever and ever, and they plodded steadily on side by side. They were wedded to their communities as well as to each other in the goal of surviving. Marriage, as Hannah knew it, was kept alive with mutual caring for each other in the never-ending struggle.

By contrast, many of Belle's friends in Montreal seemed to have married almost as strangers, with the possibility of love eventually developing, and maybe even friendship as well. The marriages in Montreal seemed almost cousinly compared to those on the coast. And Hannah smiled as she recalled the way Belle's friends — long-married couples — often talked in brotherly-sisterly clucks to each other or with sibling-like biffs of reproval over this little fleck or that little flaw.

John stirred and shifted, coming face to face with Hannah.

"I used to wonder sometimes if Cynthia might one day just decide not to come back, especially when the novelty of her northern experience had worn off — once she had proven something to herself, perhaps only that she could survive away from the stifling wealth of her family. Actually, you know, Cynthia stayed at the Bight through only one winter. That was enough for her. 'Barren and bleak,' she'd say. 'No ambience. No sophistication. No culture.' Still, she seemed to enjoy teaching the children. And in our own perhaps cool and distant way, I suppose we loved each other. But I used to wonder why she always said she'd never want to have children. I'd love to have had a houseful of sons and daughters." And as he was speaking, one of his fingers tenderly traced Hannah's fingers, down into the soft little spaces between.

John looked at Hannah's hand as he lovingly felt its form. She turned her eyes to study his face.

"Sure, I can understand why Cynthia thought I spent too much time looking after the sick. Often I was just too exhausted to discuss ideas with her, to listen to music. She used to tell me that my preoccupation with the sick was a sickness in itself. You see, at first she wanted me to be a professor somewhere in the deep South. But I had become intrigued with the North when I was a student at Annapolis

College. I used to come north along the Labrador and Newfoundland coasts on our naval exercises. It was on one of these trips I met Cynthia, when she was in her second year of volunteer teaching at the Bight.

"I know it wasn't easy for Cynthia," he said. "I'll never forget the time she tried to make bread using yeast. She was determined she would one day make a perfect loaf of bread. Every night she set the bread to rise and every morning there it sat, the same unrisen ball of dough. Then she would toss it out in the garbage. But one day she tossed the dough into the stove, hoping it would burn up quickly. The round black lids of the stove were wavering drunkenly on top of the great white puffballs of the rising dough. We had to laugh. Then Abigail, the housekeeper, put her big arms around Cynthia and said, 'You see, my maid, the bread's s'posed to go into the h'oven, not the stove.'"

Hannah shivered and crawled under one layer of blanket, though it meant thinning out the layers between her and the floor.

Hannah's comforting presence quickened John's memories of his marriage. It was as though by talking about it he was coming closer to realizing it was over. And he recalled one of their last times together.

"I'd just come back from a week up the coast to find Cynthia having a quiet Sunday read in bed. The room smelled like a scented garden. She loved to recreate her southern world. She told me about her week. I told her about mine. Then suddenly the softness of dusk was shattered by a clash of cymbals. A bass drum. The hearty blare of trumpets and trombones. And there, below our window, was the Salvation Army singing, 'Will Your Anchor Hold in the Storms of Life?'

"She flung open the window and without even looking, hurled her slipper, hitting the bass drummer on the head. He just smiled at her and carried on — with his hat pointing over one ear. Now Cynthia and I both have great respect for those splendid salvationists. But she'd come to the end of her road in the North. The more I think of my relationship with Cynthia, the more I realize it was a case of two lonely people from far away who happened to be in the same place at the same time."

"A case of happenstance?" Hannah suggested.

"I think that's the word for it," John nodded in agreement.

John wanted to say something more but he stopped himself. After a while Hannah felt his head slip from his propping elbow and fall onto her arm.

Hannah drew the covers up around John's shoulders against the increasing cold. She looked at him, tumbled in sleep against her arm. At that moment she saw his foot shoot out, as though he were jamming it down on the brake of a car. Hannah thought how strange it would seem to see John behind a steering wheel, so accustomed was she to seeing him either at the helm of a boat or scooting along as he drove a dog team. As she gazed lovingly down at him, Hannah also fantasized what he would look like in a three-piece suit, shirt and tie, or dressed in a dinner jacket at a formal event after a conference with his medical colleagues.

Feeling cold and tired, she gently lifted his head from her arm so she could put the last of the wood on the fire. Then she blew out the lamp and slipped back under the covers next to John's warm body. She felt his arm rise slowly up to rest lightly, warmly, on her shoulder.

Chapter Nine

With the rising of the winter sun, the dogs began to howl, waking Hannah and John, who felt stiff and cold from sleeping on the hard floor. John sat up and looked at Hannah, who was yawning and stretching from the short night of sleep.

"You look just like a child when you wake up," John said. He kissed her gently and slowly on the lips, as though to carry her away with him forever.

They went to the door and looked out on a beautifully snowy, silent world sculpted into windswept caves and swirls of white meringue peaked to a sugary confection.

Hannah's gaze was fixed on one tiny crystal of snow, a sparkling scintilla catching the morning light. She pointed it out to him.

"Look, it's like a little star, a bit of heaven fallen down to earth, like last night," she said.

John looked into Hannah's azure eyes. "You can see something beautiful wherever you are."

While John went to cut wood for the next surviving traveller, Hannah tidied the cabin and made notes to herself about supplies to be replaced the next time a team was passing by. Lamp oil, food, more blankets.

John harnessed the howling dogs to the komatik and brought the team to the door. Together they hauled out the box and while John lashed it in place, Hannah jammed the door shut with the wedge of wood. They stood for a moment gathering the adventures of the last twenty-four hours into one unforgettable memory. But their moment of reverie was cut short by the restless dogs.

"I don't know what's got into these creatures this morning, Hannah. They act as though they're possessed by a demon. I know they're hungry, but I've never seen them as crazy as this."

The travellers were not very far from the tilt when the dogs broke out into even greater chaos. Then with a sudden sharp lurch to the right, they jerked the sled, sending John and Hannah flying off into a deep bank of snow.

"What the devil's got into these beasts?" John said as he ran off into the midst of the dogs now snapping viciously at each other as well as their driver. Just at that moment he saw a large bloodstain on the snow.

"Something's happened here! An accident of some kind!" John shouted.

As Hannah struggled to drag herself out of the snowbank, her immediate concern was for Haim and Daniel. She wondered if they had set out during the storm to make sure she was safe.

John had all he could do to control the excited dogs until Hannah was back on the komatik. But just as he was about to give them their head, Hannah spotted something in the snow.

"John, what's that over there? Hold them for a second. I'll run over and see."

She came back with a few strands of bright green and red wool. "Look at this," Hannah said, studying the clue. "Seems like a dog team from the Straits side has been involved in the accident." Both Hannah and John were familiar with the custom of the drivers from the west of the peninsula — over along the Straits of Belle Isle — of distinguishing their dogs from others by tying tufts of coloured wool or bright ribbon on their harnesses.

"We'd better get going, Hannah, in case they need help up ahead somewhere. If there's been an accident. . ." Just then John saw something dark in the snow a few yards away from the trail.

While John controlled the dogs, Hannah ran over and picked up a small black book and then came back to the sled, looking inside the cover for somebody's name.

"Look, John, it's a priest's prayer book," Hannah said anxiously. "I wonder if this could belong to Angie's brother. He's a priest in the Straits, you know! Angie said he was coming down for the baby's birth. Dear God, let him not have been. . ." And she looked once again at the massive spillage of blood on the snow. "Has the innocent blood of a lamb been spilled by somebody's beastly dogs?" Hannah asked rhetorically. "If it's her brother. . . Oh, poor little Angie!"

They set off at top speed, John calling a steady "Siss, siss, siss" to the dogs. They were just outside the Cove when they met a team going south. John drew the dogs up to a stop and hailed the driver. It turned out to be Ben Brack, the Cove's perpetual bachelor.

"There's been an accident back down there. Do you know anything about it?" John asked.

Ben nodded slowly and sadly. "Seems like a priest was goin' south to Abel's Eye to see his sister. She was going to have a baby. Snow was so deep that the dogs had a like not to haul the driver and the priest any farther, see. Well, the priest thought he'd keep the dogs going if he ran in front to lead them. Turned himself into a carrot for they dogs. They took his body back to the Straits this morning. I expect you saw his tatters o' clothing down by the way?"

"We saw his prayer book and the blood on the snow," said John, shocked at the tragedy.

* * *

Knowing that Haim and Daniel were safe, Hannah and John decided to see Ky Henson on the way home. Twyla Henson opened the door. Her lean, gaunt body was clothed in a grey woollen skirt and a hand-knit sweater to match. Her grey hair was drawn tightly back into a little bun at the nape of her neck.

"Come in, now, come right in," Twyla said, making room for them to enter. "Was it not terrible news of the priest being et by the dogs just now? Have ye heard anything further about it? Details, like?"

"Nothing more," Hannah said patiently, for she saw Twyla as a kind of interviewer. Had there been a newspaper in the Cove, Twyla would have been a natural reporter. As it was, she was a part of the entertainment.

Some families, following an old trick handed down from one generation to another and designed to send away unwanted visitors, rattled the dishes when they saw Twyla approach. Then she would say politely, "Oh, I hear you're at tea so I'll not stay now. I'll come back again." But often she stayed long enough, standing just inside the door, to give and gather the latest news to drift over the Cove to settle where it might.

In most communities Twyla would be considered eccentric by any standards. But the people of the Cove were used to her ways. Hannah watched John look on in amazement as Twyla reached up to let down two chairs from the ceiling where they were suspended by a system of ropes and pulleys. Keeping her chairs up out of the way was a habit she had acquired when her twelve children were all living at home and the floors were often covered with beds, mattresses and feather-filled shakedowns.

Hannah and John sat down on the two chairs while Twyla settled herself in a large rocking chair. She rocked slowly back and forth, while her bare feet made their own excursions in a pair of overly large men's boots. On the chilling January morning, Hannah thought the woman's bare, blue-veined legs had a look of naked whiteness that revolted her yet filled her with compassion.

"Twyla, dear," Hannah said, "do you remember I called in one Sunday afternoon a few weeks back about the matter of Ky's coughing? Remember?"

Twyla nodded.

"Well, Dr. John is passing through the Cove this morning and he's come to examine Ky. Is he here or up in the Cove somewhere?"

"Ky's not here. He's gone down to the Bay to his brother who's some sick. He's got a bad canister, a tumour growth in his neck. I don't know when he'll be back. But I thought Ky seemed some better recently. Except for a few set-tos of coughing up bloody spittle."

John went out to the medical box and brought back a sputum collection box. He explained to Twyla that she had to get the specimen from Ky and send it up to the hospital. If it showed there were tubercle bacilli in it, then Ky would have to be admitted.

Outside John asked Hannah to keep after the Hensons until they sent the sputum. "If he has TB and refuses to come to hospital, I may have to bring a court injunction against him. Force him to be admitted. He can't be allowed to spread the disease to innocent people."

Hannah and John moved on through the village, where the people, standing in little dark knots, talked in whispers and hushes about the dead priest.

Chapter Ten

When they came to Hannah's home, John tied up the dogs and Hannah went on inside.

Daniel sat alone at his breakfast. At the sight of his mother, he dropped his spoon and stood up. "Did ye hear, Ma? A priest was eaten by dogs. Oh, Ma dear, what a thing for that poor man. It has made me feel sick right down inside."

Hannah said a few soothing words to the boy and then asked, "Where's your pa this morning, my son?"

"Pa's gone to the woods, but I stayed home with Gran'-morna because she's poorly. Not out of bed at all this morning."

"Dr. John's outside tying up his dogs. He's coming in to see Ma."

"He is? He's here? Ma, do ye think he'd draw me a pattern for a new mat I'm ready to start hooking?"

"Why don't you ask him, my son? See what he says," Hannah replied, turning to go into her mother's bedroom.

"Oh, and Ma, now that the doctor's here, maybe he could go in and see Aunt Emma. She can't hook or weave for a poorly finger. It's swollen right up like a sausage."

"I'll tell the doctor," Hannah called back.

She found her mother in a mood of sweet resignation. The old feisty, salty self was nowhere to be seen that morning. As one midwife to another, Hannah told her mother about Angie's delivery and the struggle home through the storm, but her mother showed no interest. Hannah combed her mother's hair, helped her wash and put on a fresh nightgown.

"The doctor's in the Cove this morning, Ma. I asked him to come in to see you."

Morna pulled herself painfully up on one elbow to a better vantage point for speaking her mind. "I'll not be going up to any hospital, Hannie. What I need now is for someone to work a spell on me," she said in a husky half whisper. "Someone to use a charm. But you and doctor don't hold with that kind of medicine. Do ye?"

"There's more than one kind of healing, Ma. Dr. John offers his kind of help."

Hannah heard John out in the kitchen promising Daniel that just as soon as he had examined his grandmother he would draw a scene for a mat Daniel wanted to hook.

Partway through John's examination of Morna, Hannah left the room to give her mother privacy to talk to John of anything that might be on her mind. Hannah went back in the kitchen. She made breakfast for John and opened a treasured jar of partridgeberry jam as a special treat for his toast.

Over breakfast with Hannah and Daniel, John said, "It's probably cervical arthritis that's causing your mother's headaches. She should come to the hospital for X-rays."

"I'll do my best to take her up to you, but you know how she feels about hospitals. By the way," Hannah added, "Daniel tells me Emma Speke next door has an infected finger. Maybe we could slip in and see her."

Just then Morna called out from her bedroom, as though adding a postscript to her conversations with John and Hannah, "I'll not be going up to the hospital. Ye can't soodle me into going either." Then she gave a string of puppy-like sneezes.

John looked at Hannah and said, "I wonder if your mother's catching a cold."

Hannah smiled and shook her head. "Snuff," she said quietly.

"Oh?" said John, his voice rising in interest in the way of someone who has heard of a custom and now unexpectedly sees it in practice. Not that the use of snuff was unfamiliar to him. When he was at college some of his friends had formed an Up To Snuff Club which met every Tuesday night to discuss ideas and to sneeze frequently into their grey silk handkerchiefs which they liked to keep tucked up their sleeves. It was simply that he found Hannah's mother to be an unlikely user of snuff. Then he added, "Why not? I sometimes think that the young take all the exciting practices at a time of life that's exhilarating enough. It's the old who need the new thrills."

Hannah smiled mischievously at John now starting to draw a design for Daniel. "Is that how you mean to live in your old age?" she asked.

"That's what I have in mind — all kinds of new thrills," John said, looking up into her face with expectation.

John patiently sketched a scene which Daniel would use as a pattern to hook into a mat, drawing narrow strips of old stocking and lingerie, dyed in brilliant colours, through the tiny holes in the piece of burlap or sturdy sacking. It was usually the job of the man of the house to anchor the mat to its wooden frame ready for hooking. The mats, with their scenes of fishing and sealing and ice-bergs, provided a bright, warm spot on the floor for a foot coming out of bed first thing on a cold wintry morning.

John sat at his task with the air of a serious school boy. Daniel laid his head down on the table, playing a game of "no peeking" until finally John held up his artistic creation — a sketch of a tilt with a woman standing in the doorway. Nearby stood a man with a load of firewood in his arms and behind him, a team of dogs and a komatik. John winked at Hannah and handed Daniel the drawing.

Daniel looked from the drawing to John and his mother. "Look at this, Ma. Isn't this summat wonderful? It's the best picture I've ever had for hooking. By the way, Dr. John, can you come for Sports Day next month, or maybe the big time in April?"

"I'll try," John said, putting a friendly hand on Daniel's arm. And he and Hannah stepped out into the beautiful clear day to see Emma Speke.

The Spekes' home was perched at an odd angle up on a rise of rocks above a communal garden running between the two neighbours. Hannah and Emma tended the garden, whose soil Haim and Noah had gathered from the shore in a dory to deepen its sparse depths. Every June the men fertilized the garden with tiny silvery fish called capelin, which conferred a fishy flavour on the cabbages, turnips, beets and potatoes.

The white paling fence surrounding the house looked as though its task were to hold the little lawn and the house back from tumbling into the sea. Lyddie, one of Emma's daughters, stood at the window waving to Hannah and John.

Noah Speke opened the door. "Come in now," he said. "I'm soon off to the woods, but the Missus is here."

Inside the porch they passed the sweet-smelling lumber which came up from the South by boat and stood ready for Noah's hammer to turn into coffins — his service to the community.

Noah walked ahead of Hannah and John and came suddenly to a stop. It was as though he had come to the period at the end of life's sentence. Noah carried about him a sweet air of melancholy, perhaps because of his close association with death.

Emma was nowhere to be seen in the kitchen where the freshly laundered clothes hung from a system of wooden racks strung up to the ceiling by a pulley.

Most of the women dried their own clothes in a back room, out of sight of the men. But Emma's blue drawers hung beside Noah's long, grey Stanfield "union suit" with its trapdoor drooping down at the seat.

Like the other women in the Cove, Emma boiled the clothes on top of the stove, stirring it with a sturdy wooden stick. Monday was the customary day for laundering, but Emma found one day as good as another.

Mingling with the smells of laundry and lumber was the musty, acrid odour from a clutch of hens clucking as they fluffed out their feathers and strutted about their winter enclosure in one corner of the kitchen.

In the summer the hens lived outside in a pen under the porch. But in their indoor winter life they sometimes took small jumps, boldly clearing the low railing of their enclosure to wander through the kitchen. Emma often ignored the aimless wandering of a hen — until it pecked one of her short, sturdy legs and then she would turn on it.

"Mercy upon us, can't a body have its own legs?" And she would toss the feckless fowl back into its corner.

Emma supplied Hannah's family with fresh eggs and an occasional Sunday broiler. In return, Hannah made extra bread for the Spekes because Emma was no hand at kneading the dough.

"Flat-assed Methodist bread the Missus makes," Noah laughed. The Methodists were said to have flat bottoms from sitting during the prayers in their Sunday services, while the Anglicans prided themselves on kneeling.

Emma appeared from around a corner with one of her fingers bundled up in a large white handkerchief.

"Good morning to ye both," she said as Noah slipped out the door. "I guess Danny told you about my finger. But now come right on in to the parlour and have a yarn for a minute."

As they sat at a lace-covered table, Emma turned to John, her head tilted to one side. "Did you tend the poor priest, by any chance, Dr. John?"

"No, I didn't, Emma. I was down the coast when it happened."

"'Twas a terrible thing," Emma said, resting the arms of her World War II woman's air force jacket on the table. Where the service medals would have been worn, Emma had fastened a gilt pin with the slanted script *MOTHER*.

Lyddie ambled quietly in to greet Hannah and John. Her face was wreathed in a mass of reddish-brown curls. She was a large, shy girl with the mask of pregnancy. Her first baby was due in three months.

"Thanks for coming in to look at my finger," Emma said, unwinding the bandage. "It's some nuisance not to be able to work with me hands since Daniel and I've got lots o' plans in our heads."

"It looks like it's ready to be lanced," John said. And he went out to the medical box on the komatik to fetch a package of sterile instruments.

It was when John came back in that he caught sight of an elaborate mahogany coffin in the little parlour.

"What the devil is that?" he asked.

"It's for whoever goes first," Emma said defensively. "My uncle from Harbour Grace left me a bit of money and I went to St. John's to choose it."

The novelty of the coffin-in-the-Cove had long since worn off and there were many times when Emma regretted the way she had spent her money. Her youngest child, Will, was vehement about the presence of a coffin in the house.

"Get the thing out of here, Ma. It's to invite death."

No one in the Cove gave the coffin much thought now, unlike the day the monstrous mahogany box arrived on the coastal steamer.

While Noah and Haim waited for the coffin to be lowered

over the side of the coastal steamer, they told each other jokes to relieve their uneasiness. Pointing to a crate of grapefruit, Haim nudged Noah. "Look at the size of those grapefruit. 'Twouldn't take many of they to make a dozen.'" But their laughter was cut short when they saw the dark coffin swinging down until it rested athwart their two boats.

If Noah and Haim were at all embarrassed at having to hump Emma's macabre folly ashore, in front of the knot of inquisitive men gathered on the wharf, they gave no sign of it. But they silently felt that death was too steady a visitor to be tempted with a "custom" coffin.

The women of the Cove waited out their curiosity at home, preferring to spend it in a visit with Emma. One curtain after another twitched as eyes peered out.

Twyla Henson was one of the first to pay her respects to the coffin. Her broken fingernails and rough hands caught on the tufted confection of white satin lining and irritated Emma, who slowly closed the lid.

"I see you've got three looms now, Emma," John said as he deftly relieved the infected finger.

"And I can't wait to get back at me work," Emma said.

"Well, I want you to soak your finger in hot salt water as much as you can. But what on earth are you going to do with all these things you're making, Emma?" John looked at the stack of hooked mats.

"Oh, Daniel and I have a plan," Emma said with a wink at Hannah.

Chapter Eleven

The joy of coming to know John better left Hannah both happier and sadder. She was happier for the new definition of herself that John had unwittingly given her and for the feeling that she now lived with her being filled out to the edges and beyond. But having come to know John had left an unrequited craving and a gnawing hunger. And she realized that as a married woman, neither her craving nor her hunger for John could be satisfied.

Hannah's preoccupation with John often caused her to be vague and absentminded. On this particular April evening three months after her experience in the tilt, Hannah caught herself slipping two papery-dry salt cod into the knife-and-fork drawer instead of into a bucket of water to soak for the next day's meals.

During the remaining three months of the winter Hannah had lost weight, partly because there was more than the usual amount of sickness to cope with and because of her anxiety over Haim's determination to take Daniel out to hunt seals on the ice.

More than once Morna leaned forward in her rocker and said to Hannah, "Yore clothes hang like old dresses and coats that have hung on their hook for a long spell. Ye're thin enough to have the TB, girl. Better get doctor to give ye an X-ray." Morna believed in it for others, even half believing that while the mysterious X-ray machine took a picture of the body, it might also give back some kind of healing.

Hannah had no intention of leaving the Cove during the weeks that she feared Haim might take Daniel sealing.

She looked now from the dishes out to the magnificent April sunset crowning another day in the north of Newfoundland. An hour earlier she had watched dark sweeps of mauve and magenta clouds glide regally over the sun. And now the sky was changed again, draped with the majestic colours of a rich stained-glass window.

In the window's reflection she saw that Haim was sound asleep while Morna was chaffing with Daniel and Will Speke over a game of checkers.

Hannah replaced the clean dishes up on the pine shelf above her head and stepped outside to fling the soapy water down a gulch behind the dogs' pen. As she passed the pen, one lone grey dog stood up, stretched his muzzle and yowled into the night. The other dogs joined in with their last lament for the passing day. She took in deep breaths of the cold, sweet spring air and walked back into the house, swinging the empty dish pan.

She opened the little window to lighten the yeasty aroma of rising bread mingling with the heavy odour of the ferment rising from a puncheon of spruce beer, Haim's contribution to the forthcoming "time" — the annual spring dance. A few months earlier he had boiled up the spruce boughs in a great vat and turned it into a brew. Now all he had to do was skim off the bits of bark floating on its brown swell and ginger it up with a bit of Jamaica rum.

Hannah looked out the window again, this time northward toward the Bight and its hospital. She pictured the patients with their hands stretched out to receive a cup of something warm to drink. She imagined John striding up the path. How was he spending his evenings? How did he ease his loneliness?

Haim was still asleep in the rocking chair he had made

for Hannah when she was expecting her first baby, Amity. His fiddle, tuned and ready for the dance, lay on the floor beside his feet. His chin rested on his checkered shirt, still flecked with bits of bark from the day's haul of wood. His long, reddish-grey forelock — his "topknot" — tumbled down on his chest. The rest of his hair was closely cropped.

Hannah looked lovingly at Haim. She almost envied his ability to be happy for days, just looking forward to a simple event like the dance. He was snoring now. At first it was a quiet, fluttery snore like a bird trying to escape up a narrow chimney. Then the snore became loud and bubbly. He seemed to be having a dream. His right arm reached up as though to catch at a length of taut twine.

The sight of Haim in the rocker brought to Hannah's mind the halcyon days some sixteen years earlier when they counted the weeks until their first baby would be born.

For two days before Amity's death Haim and Hannah knew an exquisite peak of bliss. While Hannah sat in the rocker nursing Amity, Haim rubbed his hands over the soft, downy hair on the baby's head. They gazed at the eager lips working on the nipple of a full, round breast. They studied her eyes under the tiny arcs of fine, fair hair.

The day that Amity died Noah Speke walked into the Holt house. With his characteristic gait, he moved to an invisible spot and there he stood, perhaps an invisible period marking the end of another sentence of life. This time a tragically brief one.

Holding a brown woollen cap in his hands between two sturdy thumbs, one deformed from an injury, he said, "I'm sorry for yer trouble, Hannie, but we have to let Amity go on to her new life in Heaven. I'll make the little box, sure."

Rain beat down on the Cove the day Amity was hauled up the hill to the cemetery on the Point. It was not customary for the women to go to the graveside, so Hannah sat at a window and watched the dark twist of men make their way up the steep, rocky climb. Hannah spotted Haim in his good dark clothes walking on behind the coffin. Haim never did seem to find a healing outlet for his profound grief. It was as though he sealed over that part of himself and never let it see light again.

For Hannah the days after Amity's death held a numbing grief. She also knew a smouldering anger she never imagined she could feel — not at her mother or Emma, nor did she rail against her own personal fate. But she felt angry for women on the coast, or anywhere, who were trapped in ill health, overwork, with little hope for anything better in life.

One day her rage broke out at her mother's endless prattling of proverbs. Just once too often Morna had said, "'Tis the Lord's will. He gives and He takes away."

Hannah's eyes flared. "Who's to say it was the Lord's will? No more talk of the Lord's will. It's enough to make Christ's wounds open up. No more, Ma. No more."

In those days Morna was able to move smartly about, and at Hannah's words she stalked off to her room, closed the door and took up her snuff. In the kitchen Hannah rested her head against the comforting heat of the high warming oven that extended out over the body of the stove. Then she took up the goose wing, a great white mother wing of some goose, the kind most homes in the Cove kept to brush cobwebs out of corners. Hannah swept the black stove lids free of crumbs, then she went into her mother's room and took her in her arms, clearing their hearts of their hidden anger.

Now on this April evening Hannah watched her mother chatting excitedly with Daniel and Will Speke, whose dark heads were bent over their game of checkers. Will, sixteen, was a constant and patient companion to Daniel. They had just finished making a calendar for the month of May.

From the time when Daniel was little, Hannah had encouraged him to make a calendar for each month, thus helping him to keep step with the procession of days, weeks and months.

The boys broke out into noisy laughter as they remembered that just one year ago Daniel had made a mistake in a calendar that had sent his father out fishing on the Sabbath, a thing that was never done. Hannah was away from the village delivering a baby. Haim set off fishing well before dawn, as he did on any other day. Later that morning he came back to the wharf with a good catch, only to be mockingly received by the men of the Cove all dressed up in their dark Sunday suits and taking their customary Sabbath stroll along the water's edge before walking back to the morning service.

"I guess we'll see you on the moon pretty soon fer fishing on the Sabbath, Haim Holt!" one of the men called out.

"Guess you're a proper Canadian already, eh, Haim?" another shouted.

Now as Hannah set dishes out for the next day, she looked at Daniel, his dark, curly hair shiny in the lamplight. She listened to his happy laughter as he shared a joke with Will, and she thought back to a day earlier that spring when Haim had said he wanted to take the boy along in the seal hunt.

Chapter Twelve

One week before the men were to go sealing, Hannah and Haim had argued once again about Daniel's future. "Ye're making a woman out of the boy with makin' pictures, weavin' and such. It won't put food on the table. He'll be a land crab doing toshy, foolery things. Don't arg with me anymore on the matter, Hannah. Don't heedle me again on the situation. No more, Han."

But Hannah pointed out that arts and crafts were no more a woman's work than a man's. "'Twas a good thing the early artists in Italy painting the holy pictures of Jesus Himself didn't think they were doing women's work, sure," Hannah said.

"Well, Daniel's going anyway, Hannah. 'Twill make a man of him. You'll see."

It was late in the afternoon when Hannah came back into the Cove on a dog team to see Haim and Daniel coming up from the wharf. Daniel was running just as fast as he could, Haim walking angrily behind.

Hannah walked into the house a few minutes after Haim and Daniel. Emma, who had been brought over to look after Morna in Hannah's absence, stood silently stirring something at the stove. Daniel was sitting near the kitchen table. His troubled head was bowed and he kept folding his grey, knitted balaclava until it was a small, tight ball.

Haim stood with his back to everyone and Hannah could tell he was furious from the red rising up his neck. Sensing the wind was up, Morna asked Emma to help her to her room. And then Emma, her neighbourly services done, discreetly left the Holts to settle their differences.

"Just what's going on here with the two of you, anyway?" Hannah asked.

Daniel looked up at his mother, his face smudged with tears. His eyes were red.

"Don't eat no more seal meat, Ma," he said in a tense, tight voice. "Ye're only eatin' death when you do. No more pie made from little seals' flipper paws. Ma, listen, it's death so women can wear their fur coats."

Neither Haim nor Hannah had ever heard Daniel raise his voice before and they stood transfixed. But Haim was equally angry. He wheeled around to stand with his feet wide apart, his arms straight at his sides, his fists clenched. He looked from Hannah to Daniel with a scunning glance. Then he shook his head. "Oh, fer the Lard's sake!" And he stormed out through the door into the chilling wind.

"Pa can't make me go sealing again, Ma. He can't make me," Daniel said, shuddering. "'Twas a proper sickener. The baby seals cried like the baby Jaisus. They wiggled and they cried. Their skins were pulled off like sweaters. And there they were, piled up in a steaming heap like baby lambs. It was some terrible, Ma. No more seal flipper pie. No more!"

Hannah was beginning to feel sick herself, but she reached for her knitting.

"Where were Noah and Will this morning?" she asked.

"They were off with a different crew. And 'twas just as well, Ma, for I had to fight it out by myself. It was my time to say summat for me, Daniel Holt. But the throw-down came over this one little seal, Ma. See, Pa was scuttling after this one little seal. He'd hit the seal once and the little fellow was bleeding from a spot on his head. Blood running down all over his white coat. Then see, this little guy looked up at me, his eyes begging for mercy. Black eyes. Like plumpy prunes. Little black whiskers. . . ."

The only sounds in the kitchen came from the yellow clock snipping off the moments of life, and from Morna's room where the earlier short sneezes had given way to the drumroll of snoring, ending periodically in a shudder, like a train convulsing to a stop on a siding.

Daniel sank down onto a chair and, resting one elbow on the table, took in a long breath. "That's not all, Ma. When that one little seal looked up for mercy and Pa had his pole up ready to strike it, I fought Pa off. I fought me own pa. And then summat else. I threw his pole as far into the ocean as I could throw it." His voice high with rage, Daniel pounded his fist on the table. "You've no idea how strong I was then, Ma!"

Hannah looked into Daniel's face. "I've seen seals killed too. I know how you feel, Danny boy. 'Tis a terrible sight." Then with a wave of her hand she gave Daniel the sign that it was time to haul out the family bathtub to the warmth of the kitchen. Together they partly filled it with warm water from the stove.

"I know Pa needs the money to pay off his fishing lines and gear," Daniel said. "And I know we use every bit of the seal for food and boots and gauntlets. And 'twas nice to have a bit of meat in March when the fish barrel was low. But I'll never go to the h'ice again, Ma."

Hannah went over to Daniel and hugged him affectionately. "You're being true to yourself, my son. But the seal hunt matters to Pa, and I love you both," she said. "You can settle with your pa when he's back. Now you'd better get on with your bath."

It was a full week before Haim could bring himself to discuss the incident.

"I was right martified, Hannah," he whispered one night in bed. "There was I in front of all the men with me own son fighting me instead o' killing the seals! The racket of it soon sent the seals sliding away and then the other men lost out on their catch too. But then didn't he throw me pole clean out into the h'ocean! And I thought Daniel's eyes were blazing. 'Twas as though he'd victor'd me somehow or t'other!"

"Haim," Hannah whispered, "that boy's just not cut out for your kind of life. Have you forgotten how he loses his balance in a boat? Slips on the fish guts. It isn't safe for Daniel to be out on those ice pans."

"I'll make myself clear, Hannah. I don't hold with Daniel doing women's work. And don't you go angelizin' on the matter, Han. Now, I don't mind if he mends up the nets a bit, knits me some socks, but fancy weavin's not going to put food on the table."

Hannah broke off the conversation with a kiss, knowing that another of Haim's crowning convictions was that a fresh glaze of his semen was the answer to any of their problems. Throughout their fifteen years of marriage, Hannah had never denied him what he considered to be his birthright. From that night on, though, there was a lingering tension in the Holt household.

At about this time, however, a new tension was also developing as Newfoundland grappled with another issue: what union with Canada might mean for them all. The island was galvanized for change. Some islanders feared for the educational system if the traditional, parochial schools should disappear. Others feared an increase in divorce, which they knew was more common on the mainland. There were still others, especially the commission-collecting merchants in St. John's — many of whom were "more British than the British" — who feared the passing of a certain elegance in life as they knew and enjoyed it. From time to time great bonfires were set up on the high, coastal hills. The anti-confederates sang an old island song, "On the Banks of Newfoundland," and a ballad which warned the people of the danger of being swallowed up by the wolfish jaws of the St. Lawrence River.

"We'd better think twice afore we turns our backs on an ocean that's fed us for hundreds of years," Morna fumed. "We'uns have to keep on thinking for ourselves and not just go along with whatever they in St. John's tell us with their silvery tongues."

She smiled wistfully to one side of her face. "They say we'll get the h'Old Age Pension — maybe thirty dollars a month instead of jest one hundred and twenty the year. There'll be handy fine Family 'llowances, what some calls the baby bonus, that'll be good for the folks with lots of lassies and laddies. Sure, and hasn't it been a nuisance to be so pore? But still we know that close to the bone's the sweetest fish!" Then Morna leaned far forward, almost coming out of her rocker. "And never forget, me lovelies, we'll still get the morning sun afore the mainlanders does!"

Morna's was a last voice crying out in the outports for the old independent Newfoundland where the elderly still held a respected place in the home and the village. She spoke for an almost imperturbable people who were slow to jump at another's whim, let alone another's bidding, unless they saw an honest human need. Then they held back nothing. Even when they had only themselves to give, they gave their all for another's need.

Hannah was proud to hear the rebel voice in her firebrand of a mother speaking up for what she believed. She looked at Will's intelligent face studying the checkerboard and realized that he was as unsuited for the seal kill as Daniel.

To raise money to buy books for the school — for the Wills and Daniels in the Cove — Hannah was pleased to read teacups or palms at the dance. She did not set much store in having what her people called the second sight. At first she only pretended to foretell people's futures. She did it as part of the entertainment. Hannah may even have seen it as a way to avoid the dusty, hearty jigs where the floor was often sufficiently crowded for a man's hand to brush unnoticed over a breast or a buttock.

At first Hannah used to make up things to "see" in the cups. And she was never far from the truth when she told someone they would soon "hear of a new baby" or take a "short trip over water" or hear tell of someone "leaving the Cove." Then little by little she predicted other events that came to pass.

When she first discovered that she could glimpse future events, she was delighted. Then she realized that any power over others was a snare for herself. Often her insight grew from information and logic. She once wrote in her diary: *When I live honestly in myself, then I glimpse the truth for me and sometimes for others also.*

All during Sports Day, a sunny February day when the people of the Cove gathered on the harbour ice to play games and take part in races, Hannah had scanned the horizon for a glimpse of John's dog team coming into the Cove. That day Hannah threw herself into the snowshoe race, sold tea and buns for a nickel and read the cups. She cheered for the dog-team races and for the man who won the contest to catch a greased pig. But by evening, when Hannah helped light the lanterns in a circle for the young people's skating party on the harbour, she gave up hope of seeing John.

Hannah was about to answer a knock at the door one evening when Noah Speke walked in, taking his measured tread. He turned his cap around in his hands and smiling shyly at Hannah, he said, "Lydd's time has come. She took sick this afternoon. The Missus says for you to come over now if ye can. The baby's coming on."

Hannah drew on her rubber boots. She had her baby bag in hand and one arm partly into her pea jacket when Morna called out, "Hold yer horses a minute, Han. I needs water for me teeth." It sounded as though her teeth were flowers needing water. But Haim knew what his mother-in-law meant and he waved Hannah on.

"I'll see to the teeth, Mar. And Dan'l and I'll help you into bed — and with anything else as is to be done."

Waving a yellow almanac, Morna said, "Haim, my boy, tryin' to help me's as much good as putting a poultice on a wooden leg." Then she added one more parting adage just for good measure. "Did ye know that when yore young, 'tis a pain to be without pleasure? But when yore old, 'tis a pleasure to be without pain!"

Hannah was almost out the door when her mother called out once more. "Mind ye say me to Lyddie. Oh, and maybe ye'd like to take her a small pinch of snuff. Nothing like a good, hearty sneeze to quicken it up at the end!"

Chapter Thirteen

Noah held his lantern out ahead of Hannah as they walked through the darkness of the night toward the Spekes' home. With the touch of shyness a short man may feel when he escorts a taller woman, Noah's hand hovered at Hannah's elbow ready to steady her if she slipped.

"Mind where ye step, Hannah. 'Tis right slippery out to-night. Just enough nip in the air to h'ice the rocks and slip your feet clear out from under ye."

But there was more than ice to be wary of as they approached the Spekes' house, for Emma had a habit of throwing out her swills to land where they might — any-where within the toss of a turnip beyond her kitchen door. The Speke home, perched up on the rocks, was ablaze with light from the extra lamps lighted when a baby was about to be born. And as the two neighbours made their way over the slippery path, Hannah was glad to be away from the recent tension of her daily domestic fuss-go-round. She knew, however, she was only trading one set of hot smells for another.

She welcomed the misty spring air drifting damply against her face like a piece of gossamer cut from a cloud. Out on the Point the faithful foghorn blew its doleful double notes of ominous warning to seafarers. Something primitive stirred within Hannah whenever she heard those sonorous signals because she pictured herself on a ship lost in the fog, being guided by its virile voice. She imagined the grey curls of fog rolling in over the Point and wondered if John and some of his staff would be able to make their way down from the Bight to attend the "time" being held in the Cove's community hall the next night.

Hannah took in one long, deep breath of the harbour's familiar, fishy odour and looked up at the Speke home to see Emma taking her vigil by the window. With one hand she held a lamp, while with the other she framed her face close to the glass, closing off the indoor light, to peer out into the darkness. Emma's wry neck, deformed from birth, gave her a questing, pensive look.

Inside the house the hens were making their soft night cluckings in their corner pen. Leaning against Noah's stacks of lumber for the coffins, Hannah kicked off her boots and jovially called out, "So you're going to be a granny again, Emma, my love!"

"It looks a little that way," Emma said as she reached to take Hannah's coat with a chubby hand whose fingers were bloated from hard work. The cuticles clung to the nails as though they had been sealed with a layer of wax.

"At first I thought Lyddie was too early, but seems she's on time all right," Emma said, leading the way through the house to a separate room which had been added to accommodate the family of eight children when they were all still at home. "At least Lyddie has skipped the days of lassy bread," she said, referring to the excessive weight gained by the women who in their last weeks of pregnancy sat by the stove and spread their bread too thickly with margarine and molasses.

Emma turned affectionately to Hannah just before they went into Lyddie's room. "Thanks for coming, my love. 'Tis always good to see you. We've been through some hard times together, you and I, Hannie, hard, hard times."

The two women were such close friends that they could exchange a gamut of emotions in a single glance. They were as practised as two nuns at reading each other's expressions, or as are those women whose lives have depended on their men, on their grown children, the unpredictable hand of nature and the sometimes tragic twists of fate. During many a crisis Emma and Hannah had seen each other's faces frozen in fear, as fixed as though they were gazing out from candid snapshots taken in a time of terror. But happily tonight neither Hannah nor Emma was fearful about Lyddie's delivery.

Lyddie lay deep in a soft feather mattress. So enveloped was she in its feathery folds that Hannah could hardly examine her. She knew that she needed a few lengths of Noah's lumber under the mattress to bolster Lyddie's gravid body. Fortunately, Noah had not left the birthing house, unlike most men in the village who would take off at the first mention of an impending delivery. Instead, he had settled himself in the unlighted "inside room" where Emma's coffin reigned supreme. From one side of Lyddie's bed Hannah could see Noah sitting quietly by the great coffin, swinging his hand idly on an ornate brass handle.

The steady knocking against the side of the coffin prompted Emma to shout, "Noah, stop that knocking. There's a good man. See to the water now. That it's boiling. We'll sing out to you when baby's here."

Hannah then asked Noah for a few boards for Lyddie's bed, and between them they slid firm, supportive lengths of board under her mattress. Like most women in the Cove, Lyddie was determined to have her baby in the bed in which it had been conceived. But Hannah thought the girl would have wanted to have her baby in the hospital, where her husband Jake was convalescing from a wood-cutting accident.

"I'm some glad I didn't have to go to hospital. Sure I'd

liked to have been near Jake, but he'll be home soon." Then in an embarrassed whisper she said, "I've heard tell they've a like to shave a person's private parts in the hospital!"

Noah was in the kitchen setting out the cups and plates in preparation for the tea that traditionally followed a birth when young Will Speke dashed in from the Holts' house. He was eager to be home for the arrival of his sister's child, but now he ran upstairs to his room, too embarrassed to say anything to the women.

Noah could not understand how Will could live so much of his life in the world of books. "Allus reading, thinking about books and such. Allus daydreaming about something or other. No mind for the real world of work," Noah had often said to Hannah. But Hannah, who admired Will's mind, always defended him.

With the older members of the Speke family gone from the nest, Will had a room of his own and could read long into the night, stopping only when his lamp ran out of oil or when it was time to pull on his waterproof oilskins and gather with the men at the wharf for yet another day of fishing.

In the many books that came into the Cove from the Bight and the charity bales from Canada and the United States, Will read about life on the battlefield, the desert, the jungle. He knew what it would be like to fly a plane and shoot one down. In his private domain of books, he could be a man of the world. He could be anyone he wished.

Then there was the summer Will discovered poetry. He tried his hand at Haiku and one day he gave Hannah a verse.

A summer's day of books
Will feed a soul more than
Many bowls of fish.

It was close to dawn when the baby began to emerge and Hannah sighed with relief for Emma had joined Lyddie in her small, whimpering cries. Hannah remembered how

113

Emma used to both laugh and cry with her children when they were little. Lyddie raised herself up on one elbow to see her baby arrive. Then with one quick, ungoverned cry, the baby was born.

"You've a fine little boy, Lyddie," Hannah said, deftly tying and cutting the umbilical cord. She wrapped the baby in soft, warm towels and laid him in Lyddie's arms, gazing down at the mother and child.

"He's some fine, Hannie. A beautiful boy. And do you remember that morning six months ago when Aunt Morna told us all 'twould be a boy? Remember the morning your ma dowsed to find out if it would be a girl or a boy?"

When she was in the mood, Morna would dowse for the answer to many a question: Should I marry so and so? Will I get to take a trip to the mainland? Will my baby be a girl? Morna had sometimes even suspended her dowsing ball over the body of someone who was sick in order to locate the troubled area.

She used the ball as a divination tool and had devised her own system of interpreting the way the ball turned — clockwise, counterclockwise or simply swinging with a neutral opinion back and forth. Sometimes Morna put a piece of a person's hair in the hollow ball to act as "the witness." It was an art Morna had learned from an old Indian woman who once visited the Cove from the Labrador. Soon after Lyddie knew she was pregnant, Morna had suspended her dowsing ball over her unborn baby. "'Tis a boy from the way the ball turns, sure," Morna had said, watching the little blue glass ball making its circle around and around. . . .

Emma hurried in with a basin of warm water and bathed the baby while clucking the oft-repeated and loving caveats by which each child in the Cove was communally cared for, cherished and at the same time controlled.

"We'll keep ye from the boo-darbies, sure!" she said,

sending the water up in little warm waves over the baby's round middle. "The bad fairies'll never get you, my son."

The adults in the Cove echoed each other's common concern for the safety of the young with the half-playful, half-serious threats that they preferred to physical punishment. The more severe the threat, the less likely it was to be carried out. Dark places, narrow lanes, graveyards, empty buildings, hollows, marshes or barrens could all be the home of "the headless man" or some other frightening, eldritch creature. The more dangerous the place — and there were always the hazardous, rocky heights with the ocean waiting below — the more terrifying the threatening monstrosity.

As Hannah listened to Emma initiating the newborn baby into the village's system of safety, she thought of how often Morna had sounded the same tocsins in Daniel's ears.

"If ye don't behave," Morna was fond of saying jokingly to the young Daniel, "I'll knock ye into the middle of next week!" Or she would threaten to show him the four corners of the room. When Daniel was older, she would give him thimble pie, which began with a tug on the ear followed by a smart thump on the boy's head with her thimbled finger. Morna and Haim had a tacit agreement about correcting Daniel's manners and mores. And when Morna played mother to Daniel, he rewarded her with a compliance which she had never received from her daughters.

In the outport network of raising a child, there was a control for every human transgression. If a boy was found masturbating, he was warned that either he would go blind or his hand would fall off. But any child with an inkling of insight soon reasoned that there were few blind men about and that the same hand was in no apparent danger when it set out to help the same part of his anatomy with its other natural functions.

Hannah knew that the myths of her childhood were

woven right into the imaginative realm of her mind, the part that wrote in her diary each day, that was her companion when as a child she had stayed out alone after dusk and dared to look under an overturned boat or to investigate a tall, shadowy "figure" standing between two great rocks. Hannah often filled herself with such terror that it was a relief to hear Morna call, "'Tis supper time, Hannie. Come in now afore the boo-darbies get ye!" How pleasant she found it to run into her mother's kitchen to the warm, familiar pleasures: the yellow light radiating from the oil lamp, the cool, green smoothness of the oilcloth table covering, the places set for everyone, and the savoury drift of food soon to be served. It was the time of day when Hannah wrote in her diary, when the demanding gods of the day — turning fish, making soup, cleaning house — were appeased, and the god of the night came down with the dark. . . .

With the remnants of the birth cleared away, Emma called out to Noah and Will to come see the baby. Noah's face looked as though it were lighted from below with a gentle candle of love.

"What a great little fish-gaffer he is, Lyddie, my maid," said Noah as he stroked the baby's head.

Lyddie shifted restlessly on her bed of boards, and Noah, sensitive to her discomfort, said, "Guess the boards are a bit hard, now. Well, let's see if'n I can get them out." When Will came downstairs from his room, he helped his father carry the lumber to the stockpile for coffins and then went back in to look at his newborn nephew.

"May I hold him a minute, Lyddie?" Will asked. And he picked up the wise-looking baby and carried him around the house.

A few minutes later Noah called from the kitchen, "Tea's ready, everyone. The Missus has some flat-assed Methodist bread for us all." Everyone laughed as though hearing his well-worn joke for the first time.

They had sat down to tea in the early dawn when out of the corner of her eye Hannah thought she saw something stirring outside the window. She slipped over to the door. Peering out through a small window into the mists of the morning, she saw Daniel. Quickly she gave him a sign which he knew meant to "wait back for a minute."

Hannah then returned to her place at the table, and cocking her head to one side, as though to listen to a faraway sound, she said, "Did anyone hear a knock at the door? I coulda sworn I did. I'll go out and see." And before anyone else could stir, Hannah opened the door. Such was the love Hannah had for Daniel that she would always spare him embarrassment.

"Why, Daniel, my son, come right on in! You must ha' met the stork on your way. Lyddie's got a fine boy. And you're just in time for tea."

Daniel was relieved at the way his mother covered the pain and confusion they both felt from his venture with voyeurism. The boy took off his boots and went with Hannah into Lyddie's room.

"Ye've got a fine baba, Lyddie," Daniel said, pulling back the baby's covers to curl its tiny fingers around his own. He nodded his head as he gazed spellbound at the infant nursing at Lyddie's breast.

"'Tis summat wonderful," Daniel said, sipping tea at the table. "He looks just like the pictures of the baby Jaisus." Then more to himself than to anyone else, he added, "Maybe Jaisus was a Newfoundlander in a way."

Noah sensed Hannah's disquietude and picked up the slack in the conversation while Emma offered more tea all around.

Hannah and Daniel walked home arm in arm over the slippery rocks. The first hint of a rosy dawn struggled through the thinning fog hanging over the Point. The foghorn still blared forth the only two notes in its repertoire, and a lone gull circled and rose down by the wharf.

They walked on in silence until they were close to home, when Daniel slowed down his pace. Turning to Hannah, he took her hand in his and looked into her eyes.

"I know it was wrong, Ma, to stare through the window watching ye born Lyddie's baby, the way I did."

Hannah felt a deep poignancy for Daniel who, at the tender age of fourteen, was feeling vulnerable to the mysteries of the adult world he was entering.

"One day, Daniel," Hannah said, "you'll meet a young woman you'll love. Someone who'll love you just as much as you love her — just as much as I love you, but in a different way. It'll happen."

They stood together that morning on the stony path, a mother and her son, talking of life's most precious gift, the gift of love, while behind them a new Newfoundland baby was thriving on its first earthly breaths, and the sun would soon shine through the April fog.

Daniel had more questions to ask. "How do you know when you're in love with somebody, Ma? What does it feel like and all?"

"Sometimes love takes you quickly and other times it comes over you like a feeling of comfort wrapping itself 'round you — like when you come into the warm of your own home after being out in a storm. It's like coming home to all that there is of yourself and finding there's still more beyond what you thought you were. You feel alive all the way through and find only the best in yourself — and in others. Because, Daniel, when someone loves you, they see only the good in you, just as you bring out the best in them."

Hannah led the way into their home. They could have talked longer on the topic of love, but Hannah was careful lest she deprive Daniel of his own experience of love in the springtime of his life.

Daniel was not long in falling asleep and Hannah was partway up the ladder to her bedroom when she realized she was too wide awake to sleep. Rather than lie at Haim's slumbering side, she decided she would make a pilgrimage to the Point, where she could watch the sun come up.

Hannah revelled in the freedom of the cool, fresh dawn air. She felt as though she were off on an unexpected furlough, and she moved along at a steady pace, her rubber boots scrunching over the loose gravel, carrying her out to the heights of freedom.

Chapter Fourteen

Hannah hurried through the sleepy village in the early dawn of the day, eager to fill her being with the sight of the open, swelling sea and to feel the mighty sweep of the wind high up on the Point. There was just enough snow to be packed into iciness on some parts of the path. In other parts the path was bare and the sound of Hannah's rubber boots was accompanied by the beating of the waves against the boulders at the water's edge.

Here and there an occasional lamp burned in a home, perhaps to light the way for a fisherman dressing to go out for the day's catch of cod, or for someone awakened by a restless bladder, the machinations of a melancholic mind, or the nudging of a lively libido.

Well above and beyond the houses now, Hannah turned and walked backward to gaze down on her village lying like a small mediaeval fastness against a grey rind of rocky ramparts. She felt again, as she always did when she was a few hundred yards away, a rising tide of compassion and pure love for her family and the people in the Cove. Away from the Cove, Hannah renewed her appreciation of their strength, tempered by gentleness, their sense of honour, chivalry, courage and durability as knights of the sea and the snow.

On this April morning Hannah thought especially of

Haim. She kicked the gravel in frustration as she reflected on his struggle with the balance that always weighed against him when they did his bookkeeping together. With the old system of depending on the local merchant for credit, the yield of a year's work was often only that of further financial slavery. Despite the fact that Haim worked harder every year and cleaned his fish meticulously to get the highest possible market price from the fish merchants, he was always in debt. She understood why he was determined to have Daniel's company in the lonely, relentless struggle to keep his head above the poverty line.

Hannah looked back at her house with its thin twist of smoke rising from the little chimney. The season's sealskins were hung against one wall, espaliered to tautness in their frames like quilts in the making. This spring's skins, next winter's boots and mitts. Behind the house Haim's old fishing boat lay overturned beside the new one whose still-uncovered ribs curved up into the air like the sun-bleached skeleton of a beached whale. Hannah always marvelled that each fisherman could build his own boat, his komatik and even his house.

Her gaze turned toward the frame school standing beside the church — appropriately enough since religion was their common platform. Whatever else may have gone unlearned, all of the graduates of the little schoolhouse knew the catechism by heart before they left its one spartan room with the smell of linseed oil, damp wool, whiffs of urine and the odours peculiar to each child and his home. Often a haze of wood smoke drifted out from the stove to hang as thickly inside the schoolroom as did the fog floating past outside the low square windows.

The same teacher had taught Hannah throughout her years in the little school. "Old Ewart" he was called, even though he was only in his thirties. Ewart usually sat at his desk, his hands fingering a set of weights and measures, the

Holy Bible, a slender birch rod and a globe, many of whose countries were coloured a rosy pink, the colour of the British Empire, "upon which the sun never sets." Ewart's full, flushed cheeks were in contrast to the pale complexion of the Christ whose portrait, showing a band of children receiving a blessing, hung behind his desk — close to a flag, the Union Jack, whose silkiness folded down on itself.

Ewart's was no easy task because he had all of the elementary school grades to teach at one time. Many of the students knew they would not be attending school beyond the early grades and their indifference often took the form of mischief. In contrast, there were at least a few students, like Hannah, who quickly absorbed everything Ewart could teach, then hungered for more knowledge.

On many days Hannah kept a novel in her desk, in self-defence against the hour when Ewart would once more begin to reminisce about his nocturnal escapades in a Devon barracks during World War II. She concealed her reading with a generous blotter, sliding it surreptitiously down to reveal a line at a time. Then every once in a while Hannah challenged Ewart on teaching he touted as fact. There was the morning, for instance, when Ewart told the class that Cleopatra was an Egyptian. Just a few weeks before, Hannah had read a book sent down to the Cove with Cynthia Weatherton's name inscribed in the front. It's title? *Cleopatra.*

On that particular morning Hannah rose and contended Ewart's statement. "Sir," she said, "I wonder if it might not be more accurate to say Cleopatra was originally a Greek?"

The truth of the matter did not interest Ewart. He was too angry at having his authority questioned. But the subject of nationalities did trigger something in his mind. Although Ewart never took up the rod to Hannah — as he so often did to others on just as slight a provocation — he reserved for her a particularly caustic calumny against which no child had much defence.

"Well, now that we're on the subject of nationalities, Hannah Burns, you're not a true Newfoundlander yourself now, are you?" Ewart said in a taunting voice.

Heads turned to see how Hannah would react to Ewart's blow. Something like a steady wave of sheet lightning shimmered through Hannah's mind. She knew she had to speak up or forever wish she had.

"Well, sir," she said quietly, "I understand ye're from the South yourself and that your father came from the mainland."

Twenty heads turned like spectators at a tennis match to see what Ewart would say. But he simply drew himself up and turned away.

Hannah found no pleasure in her victory, but she was gratified that she had had the courage to stand up for herself. Hannah hoped that her example of responding to an indignity might encourage her schoolmates to play a role in directing their own destinies.

For most of the children in the Cove it did little good to complain about a teacher's injustices, for the parents had "small ears" for a child's school-day miseries. Most parents either ignored the youthful plea for justice and understanding or they suggested the child simply stop going to school. Some parents went so far as to repeat the teacher's beating, doubling the insult to the child.

Some years later Hannah went back to make peace with Ewart.

"I'm sorry to have insulted you or your South when I was in my last year with you," Hannah said one day on her way home from high school. "But we in the North often feel filched by the merchants in the South. I expect that anyone who comes North from the South is sure to understand that."

A few weeks later old Ewart left a parcel on Hannah's doorstep. She opened it to find a copy of Gibbon's *Decline and Fall of the Roman Empire.* Inside the three-volume case was a handwritten letter encouraging her to continue her education and to consider that when Gibbon wrote this masterpiece he had memorized every paragraph before writing it down. . . .

Hannah did not always go into the little cemetery when she walked up to the Point, but on this morning she untwisted the rusty wire on the gate and walked over to the grave of Amity. Hannah realigned the shells she had gathered to outline the perimeter of the little grave. She stood by the gravestone Belle had sent from Montreal.

Hannah was only nineteen when Amity died, but it was the time she first learned to transcend sorrow and even to know a kind of inner peace. She knew how to take strength from struggle.

As she closed the gate on the graveyard, she shivered from the bleakness of the windswept cemetery poised on its lofty glaciated height, offering up its holdings much as the ancients laid out their dead on high rocky altars for nature's agents and elements.

Hannah climbed on up to the highest peak, the place of greatest freedom, and listened to the foghorn's ominous warning, sounding as though it were a great open mouth waiting to swallow her. Through the grey fog she gazed up at a sky streaked with dull scarlet and crimson as though some painter of paradise had been practising his strokes on the morning's canvas.

Hannah stood on the topmost peak and her weariness fell away as she looked out over the great open sea, heaving like a dark-blue quilt tufted with white foam and covering a bed of restless creatures tumbling underneath.

One day she would bring Daniel here. He would stand proud and tall, making the power of the sea his own. Not for Daniel would there be boo-darbies and headless men. She dreamed too of the day she would show John the lofty height, the crowning peak of the Point.

As she inched ever closer to the edge of the cliff, Hannah saw an enormous iceberg framed in a rocky inlet below. Even in the dullness of the dawn, it seemed to light up its crystalline blueness from a source within its great mass. Twin peaks rose up from a deep cleft, as though two icebergs had been fused to create a glacial cathedral flanked on one side with frozen, flying buttresses and on the other by a castle encrusted with icy turrets and towers.

Just as Hannah leaned forward to get an even better view of the iceberg, her foot slipped on the slimy moss in a rocky pocket of wintry meltwater and she lost her balance. She almost regained her footing but a sudden sweep of wind sent her over the edge of the precipice.

In the split second of falling Hannah was terrified that she was heading toward a watery grave. But her nightmare was interrupted when she landed on a ledge of rock jutting out about six feet below the place on which she had just been standing.

As Hannah faced the sheer cliff of the rock above her, she knew she dared not take even one look down below. She heard the sea sucking hungrily at the caves well over a hundred feet directly beneath her. Looking up she saw a flock of seabirds writing their dark untidy sentence across the sky. Hannah studied the nest remnants of a puffin or a turr, tucked into the corner of the ledge. A gull circled above her head and she thought of Prometheus on the rock. Was she to be an offering on this high granite altar, to have her vital organs plucked away? The foghorn, sounding closer now, belched at her again and again. Out of the corner of her eye Hannah caught a glimpse of its sources, the lighthouse and the lighthouse-keeper's home.

It struck Hannah that if she shouted loudly enough the keeper, his wife or one of his children might hear and come to her aid. But Hannah imagined the scenario of the rescue. The ignominy of being dragged up to safety on a rope by two or three men only fired Hannah's determination to rescue herself.

The first thing she did was to jettison her heavy rubber boots; gingerly she cast off one and then the other. At the sound of her boots hitting the surface of the sea, perspiration began to trickle between her breasts. Now her gaze was riveted to the granite edge of the cliff a few inches above her face. Before her eyes the granite glowed with hints of amethyst, emerald, topaz and gold. With an alchemy she neither understood nor questioned, the colours quickened her courage.

The foghorn blew once more and, with a sudden surge of strength, Hannah grasped the granite edge and her strong arms pulled her body upward until she could swing one foot and then the other over the top to safety.

She crawled commando-style away from the edge and rolled over on her back in sheer relief, looking numbly up at the mottled sky. The mournful foghorn no longer played her dirge. With a thankful heart she drew herself up to her feet and taking a cautious glimpse at the ocean, saw her rubber boots riding out to sea on the waves like the tiny Wellingtons of a toy sailor.

In the excitement of her self-rescue, Hannah had not noticed any pain, but now her hands were stinging from cuts on the palms where they had gripped the sharp edge of the cliff.

As she ran down the mountainside with both hands bleeding, her limbs ached with fatigue. Close to the Cove, Hannah slipped down to the water's edge and knelt to clean the mud from her clothes and wash the blood from her hands. She sloshed the salt water on her face and smoothed back her hair.

Just as Hannah was straightening up she heard a thunderous explosion that made the very rock beneath her seem to move. She thought it came from near the Point. Within seconds fresh new waves rode in over the rocks and she jumped back to avoid being soaked. As she hurried on toward her home, she remembered having seen the iceberg with its deep cleft. She felt certain the earth-shaking boom had been caused by the huge iceberg capsizing and breaking in half, a phenomenon she had witnessed once before.

The explosive noise brought the people of the Cove to their windows and into the road, where they nodded at the uncommon sight of Hannah scooting along in her stocking feet. Little did they know, she mused, that she had just escaped her second brush with death in the last three months — the first in the January blizzard with John and his dog team.

Arriving home, however, Hannah feared the worst as she opened the door and faced her family. Morna sat in her rocking chair looking grim. Daniel was dutifully working the risen dough at the kneading table, but as soon as he saw his mother, he rushed over and hugged her in relief. Haim sat sullenly at his breakfast. He took one look at Hannah, then pounded his fist on the table, sending his saucer of tea up in little brown waves.

"Been to the Point again, haven't ye, Hannah? And in the dark at that!" he shouted. "We've been to the Spekes' to look for ye. We've been half drave crazy wondering where ye were. Will ye ever behave like the other women in this Cove? Are ye ever going to become a grown woman?"

Would the day ever come, Hannah wondered, when she would not have to account for her every move?

Hannah had seen the young outport women full of plans to live up to their dreams and hopes, believing that their love was unique. Never, they thought, would they take on the weary resignation of their mothers' mundane marriages. But one, two or three babies later and most of them wore the same apron of apathy. Hopes were deferred and dreams drifted out with the tide. And no one bothered to think much about the inner winds that sicken the soul when a person's deepest and dearest dreams are allowed to die.

"Yes, Haim, I've been to the Point again. I'm sorry I caused you to worry about me. But I'm home now, look."

Haim wove the tines of his fork in and out of the knee of his threadbare pants. Then he looked up. "And I see ye've had a fall at that."

"Yes, I did have a little fall. Slipped on a bit of sishy slush and took a tumble. But I'm. . ."

Haim flung his fork clear across the room. Then he stamped his feet up and down as though he were marching even while he sat at the table. It was a childish habit which in earlier years used to amuse Hannah. But later on it irked her to hear him tramping up and down with the two feet he sometimes called larboard and starboard. The tramping was a carry-over from a custom of the Cove men who drummed their feet on the church floor while they spoke, in sonorous tones, the last line of a hymn.

Haim reached for his saucer of tea and swallowed it down in one noisy gulp. Then he sneezed three times, as he often did when he was upset.

"Mind ye don't go to the Point again, Hannah. Do ye hear?"

But Hannah's fall had baptized her in a rainbow of courage and Haim's words fell away of their own weight, even as he hitched his braces up and snapped them with his next salvo.

"Most of us see the sea every day. Don't need to climb a hill to look at more water."

As Hannah was framing an answer, Morna cleared her throat.

"Hannie, if'n ye go to the cemetery alla time to visit Amity's grave, then I think it's right morbid. But if ye go to the Point for a strengthener, my maid, then I understand. I do."

Her mother's words warmed Hannah's heart. Hannah took down an enamel basin and dippered hot water into it from the stove to wash her face and hands.

"Leave a bit o' water for a person to shave hisself with, will ye?" Haim's words were banked with fury. As he took the dipper from Hannah's hand to fill his shaving mug, Hannah searched for the words that would heal the rifts in the family.

She filled her basin and looked over at Haim in his Stanfield undervest, shaving with his straight razor.

"We'll all have a happy evening tonight at the dance," she said cheerily as she started up the ladder to wash in her bedroom.

It was Morna who supported Hannah's effort to leave a little benediction over the family. "I was just thinking, Hannah, 'tis a funny thing how a fright can sharpen the mind summat wonderful. . . ."

In that moment Hannah knew what someone stranded alone on a desert island would feel like at discovering another human footprint. She looked at her mother in amazement. Had she had a similar experience that she could speak of the incident with such insight? Hannah smiled at Morna; it had been a long time since she had felt such loving understanding from her mother.

Hannah started up the ladder-stairs again. This time it was Daniel's motions that caused her to stop. He had been standing by his great bowl of dough, the sleeves of his blue checkered shirt rolled up to the elbows, his face bright with an idea. He broke off three balls of dough and walked over to his father, offering him one.

But Haim only shook his head and mumbled, "I've got my mouf full of soap already, Dan'l."

The boy had hoped to salve the wound of his Fisher King father whose plenteous catch fed others but barely nourished himself.

Daniel shrugged and walked over to his grandmother, offering her one of the lumpish balls. "Like to taste it afore it's cooked, Gran'morna?"

Morna smiled warmly and took the dough. But she did not put it in her mouth. Instead, she rolled it to make a slender length which she looped over her fingers.

"I used to be crazy for a game of cat's cradle, Daniel," she said, trying to work the dough string over her gnarled fingers. "Funny t'ing, Danny, back then the string allus got too tight, but this loopy string's too soft to hold." And so saying, Morna rolled it back into a grey ball and stuck it like a wad of chewing gum to the arm of her chair.

By the time Daniel reached Hannah, she had had time to appreciate his peace offering of bread and wine wrapped up in one yeasty, fermented lump of dough. It was his sacrament and his thanksgiving for the family, and especially for his mother's safe return.

Hannah shifted the basin of water, reaching out to take Daniel's offering. Thoughtfully she slipped the dough into her mouth.

"That's a beautiful thing to do, Daniel, my boy. God bless you." Then Hannah turned to her family. "'Twill be a happy evening tonight at the dance, sure. We'll all be laughing and singing."

Morna, who was looking forward to the annual spring dance perhaps more than any of them, came out with another of her time-worn adages: "The mood o' the morning is almost never the same as that o' the evening."

Later that morning Haim and Daniel left for the woods to cut fuel while Hannah bathed her mother and curled her hair with curling tongs heated on top of the stove. Morna wanted to have a rest to be ready for the big evening ahead. And Hannah, having been up all the night before — first with Lyddie and then at the Point — welcomed the moment when she could get into the family tub before sinking into her featherbed.

The foghorn began again to drone out its warning and from her window Hannah could see that the fog was heavy out over the Point. She thought of John, of the covenant of caring that had grown between them, and she wondered if he would make it to the dance. She longed to see him again after the three months since their night in the tilt, but she also sensed a change in her perception of both Haim and John.

The two men had once been like the two halves of a figure of eight crossing heavily over her solar plexus.

Now on this April morning the two-man figure of eight had opened out to an oval loop, the weight of its cross-over now lifted completely from Hannah. That morning after her fall and her rising again, she fell contentedly asleep, dreaming of a record turning around and around on a turntable. But there was something different about this particular platter in that the needle — instead of starting at the outside of the grooves and moving inward in increasingly small circles — began at the centre and moved outward. There was one other difference in this record player — the arm holding the needle was human.

In her dream Hannah watched with fascination as the needle, guided by the human hand, rode closer and closer to the edge in ever-widening circles. She looked again at the record and saw that the needle was now entirely off the limits of the disc but was still making beautiful music as the human arm, moving out into the spheres in ever-expanding gyres, continued to create the most exquisite music.

Chapter Fifteen

By the time the Holt family was dressed for the dance, the querulous mood of the morning was behind them. They were ready to give and take in an evening of merrymaking that flung over the walls of life whatever burdens the day, the month or the year may have held for them. It was spring again and another winter was almost behind them.

Hannah was dressed in a full, burgundy-coloured skirt that she had made for herself with a matching woollen blouse sent by Belle and still smelling of wood smoke from her Laurentian chalet. Daniel and Haim were in their next-to-Sunday best clothes: cardigan sweaters and open-neck shirts, dark trousers and rubber boots.

Morna wore her good black dress, under which she was gantried around by a tea-rose-coloured garment she called her "stays." The corset was indeed "stayed" right up to her armpits with strips of stiff whalebone. It also served as a brassiere to discipline her ample bosom. Morna got herself trussed into the garment only on special occasions. "Trims me down," she told Hannah, whose task it was to lace her mother into the corset and tie the knot on the bastille imprisoning her flesh.

Morna's stays creaked quietly as Haim and Daniel carried her in her own chair, like an Egyptian princess, out into an April night hung with fog. In her lap she held Haim's fiddle, bow and mouth organ. Daniel carried his share of the chair as well as a long pole, one end of which was tucked under his arm. On the other end of the pole hung a red oil lantern, sending out a light that was dwarfed by the dark. There were no shadows anywhere, or maybe it was all shadow. Even when the weather was clear, the darkness of a Newfoundland night could hide a path; when there was also fog, the watery roadside ditch lay ever ready for the wayfarer's foot.

Hannah walked just a little behind the trio, carrying in one arm a bowl of salad made from tinned beets and potatoes, and in the other, a dish of sauerkraut, some of which she had served her family for supper, respecting Morna's belief that it prevented a heavy head the next day. It foiled what Morna called the "Irish sulk."

The thick fog drifted against their faces like wet cobwebs; it was a little like breathing in your own breath again. The heavy dampness of the night amplified the sounds of their rubber boots on the gravel, much as a shell held to the ear gives back the sounds of the sea. Hannah felt the fog drifting across her eyes, blindfolding her with its lengths of moist grey gauze. The foghorn still bellowed out, reminding Hannah that it was not a likely night for John to be travelling down the coast.

As the Holt family walked warily through the dark, they met and joined other families peering through the fog, straining to recognize each other. Then would come the sudden, bright moment of recognition and the cheery call, "Well, well, look who's here! 'Tis Uncle Haim himself, Hannah, Danny boy and Aunt Morna Burns too!"

Only that morning they may have seen each other in the woods or out in their boats, but tonight they were like revellers at a masked ball disguised by the fog until they came within view. To each family Morna called out, "'Tis some foggy a night out here. Maybe the mauziest night I've ever seen. But takes more'n a bit of fog to stop a time!"

A time could be held in a kitchen, a store, on a sailing vessel or in a community hall if an outport was lucky enough to have one. There was dancing to the fiddles, accordions and mouth organs. There was also dining and drinking, recitations and joke telling. Often the evening stretched happily on into morning or at least until all of the barrels of spruce beer and the bottles of Newfoundland screech were empty.

For a few blessed hours the fisherfolk could forget their troubles. They tossed away their failures and gave themselves over to enjoying the evening. They would deal with tomorrow when it came. "No use to borrow trouble. Hope for the best but always keep an eye out for the worst."

"Remember Nofty," another warning went. "Nofty was up to forty when lost the pork!" Nofty, a Newfoundland card-player, had reached a score of forty in a game where the goal was forty-five. He was right up there close to winning when the "pork" got away from him.

Haim and his family were among the first to arrive at the hall. They set Morna's chair down in the main room below the head of a stuffed caribou — the island's "national animal" — mounted near the main door. Beneath its majestic branching antlers its glazed eyes stared obsessively out through the open doors into the wilderness of fog as one family after another passed under its velvety nose.

The Newfoundland outporters had a special charm, no doubt inherited from their English forebears from Devonshire or the Irish immigrants from Cork or Kerry, who had reached this "New Found World" hundreds of years ago. On this April evening the people of the Cove were like characters from the *Canterbury Tales* stopping at an inn for a brief pilgrimage of pleasure.

Hannah took the lantern from the end of Daniel's pole and hung it on one wall, lighting up part of the long hall with its platform across one end. The light sent a warm glow across a photograph of the Royal Family. There stood King George VI with his sadly serious face, and beside him his gracious smiling queen, Elizabeth. In front of them sat their children, the Princesses Elizabeth and Margaret, in their full, flossy pink dresses, their legs crossed at their white ankle socks above shiny, patent-leather shoes.

A picture or a calendar bearing the royal faces graced most homes, representing both the unity of the family and the power of the British Empire, at that time lavishly strewn around the globe. Newfoundland was proud to be a colony of the Mother Country, and the Union Jack received almost the same kind of homage as did the Holy Trinity. The Union Jack with its intersecting crosses of red, white and blue was draped near the picture of the Royal Family close to an old photograph of Ontario's famed Dionne quintuplets, dark-haired cherubs celebrating their third birthday with hallmark hugs and kisses for each other.

Haim and Daniel had no sooner set down Morna's chair when she said, "Now, my gentlemen, I have a like to sit right over there." And she gestured toward a long table where Emma and the other women were laying out the food and taking turns swirling a giant cheesecloth tea bag in a cauldron of boiling water. With Morna settled to her satisfaction, Haim and Daniel headed back to the house for their puncheon of spruce beer.

"We'll be back the once," Haim called cheerily to Hannah who was setting up a small table, two chairs and a bowl for the money that her innocent prophecies over palms or tea leaves would bring in to buy books for the children.

It did not take long for the hall to fill. The deeply lined faces of the elderly glowed under the kindly light of the lanterns. On such an evening the older members relived the dances of their youth, for there was still the same full-hearted devotion to having a good time.

The old were cherished for themselves and for the sense of balance they brought. It was the older people who shared the wisdom that every happy turn has its shadow, just as every sorrow somewhere has its lightness. The elderly out-porter and his wife knew that love, unconditional and open, was the best lamp for the path between the high times and the low. They knew that if the home is not a hearth of love, then it might become a hotbed of hostility. Understandably, the young of the Cove migrated steadily toward the timeless wisdom of their elders, many of whom appreciated the alchemy that worked in their lives when they acquired the patience to offer up their constant gratitude to God even in the face of seemingly impossible situations.

Even small babies, still warmly buttoned to the breast, were brought to the dance. Toddlers swung shyly behind their mothers' skirts. Adolescents studied each other, wondering: Is he The One? Is she The One? A dance offered the young a rare chance to be together socially; there were few other opportunities to come to know each other, aside from "walking out" after church or "grassing about" on a pleasant summer evening. And if a couple were "talking," the relationship was almost always serious.

Haim and Daniel were soon back with the beer. Haim looked over at Hannah and gave her a wink and the familiar Newfoundland nod — a quick flick of the head. Haim loved Hannah and she loved him with the devotion that flowed from her wellspring of loving kindness. She knew he was steadfast and devoted. He was honest. Haim never held a grudge. Hannah watched him passing a box of gumbeens — chewing tobacco — to Daniel, Noah and Will. "Dance away now, me lads, dance away at it," he told the boys as he stepped quickly up to join the other music-makers on the platform.

Here and there in the community hall that night Hannah

recognized items of clothing that had come to the Cove from Belle in Montreal or the charity bales from the mainland via the Bight. Some of the clothes were out of style. Hems had gone up and down; waists had gone in and out. A little jacket from Paris, trimmed around with passementerie, and fitting neatly up under the arms, might be mated with a home-made skirt. A Woman's Auxiliary Air Force cap might be borne proudly aloft above a pair of sturdy rubber boots. Any change in the wardrobe was a distraction from the constant grind of poverty.

Most of the women wore dark colours and "Mary blue" was one of the most popular. Bright red, considered to be the colour of the hussy, was seldom worn.

Hannah gazed expectantly out over the crowd. Try as she would, she could not put Dr. John from her thoughts. She wanted to tell him about her experience out on the Point. He would understand what transformation had come over her during that traumatic fall.

Hannah watched the young men and women pay their respects to her mother. Young brides, still blushing easily, came to Morna for a word of advice, approval, encouragement. Antedating Hannah as the local midwife, Morna had delivered many of them. She had seen them grow from pink-lipped babies to young women battening on motherhood. Young males, grown from being whingeing babies to strapping bears of men, lingered by her chair to say a few words and to listen to the anecdotes the young never tire of hearing about themselves — and Morna never wearied of telling. She remembered their biographies as clearly as she recalled crimping crepe paper flowers for their christenings, their weddings and their parents' funerals.

When the music-makers played a soulful piece about a Newfoundland youth going off to World War I, Morna started to sing at the top of her lungs. Then, just as suddenly, she stopped. Hannah watched uneasily as Morna's tongue rummaged under her dental plate for a trespassing partridge-berry seed. Her false teeth rose dangerously close to falling from her lower lip. "Store teeth," as they were called, were not easy to replace in the Cove and Hannah breathed a sigh of relief when the truant seed was evicted, the dentures were back in place and Morna's high wavering notes soared out over them all once again. Hannah then simply turned her mind to enjoying the evening and she joined in dancing the jigs and the reels with the best of them.

At one point Noah came shyly up to Hannah and asked her to dance with him. The moment Haim saw them dancing, Noah's boots rubber-stuttering along the floor, he dropped his fiddle and hustled across the hall to sweep Emma away from her post at the food table. One by one the rest of the dancers left the centre of the floor to form a ring around the popular foursome. Hannah towered above the other three like an elegant Maypole around which they danced. The music speeded up and the foursome danced faster and faster while the circle of admiring friends clapped in glee and the men stamped their boots to the music.

At the end of the dance Haim turned from Emma to Hannah and, lifting her off her feet, twirled her around until her hair came tumbling down over her slender shoulders.

Then the four dancers left the floor amid calls, cheers and the wild, lone warbling of Morna's voice clinging valiantly to the last note.

Emma stopped by Morna's chair. She put her arms around her beloved neighbour and life-long friend.

"You're in fine voice tonight, my love," Emma said.

"Ah, I loves to sing to they old reels and jigs. I'm not allus on key but I'm some lusty tonight!" Then Morna covered her mouth with her hand and whispered, "Mind ye don't tell Hannah, but I think I'm getting a bit highly up! 'Tis the finest kind of beer, sure!"

Then Morna reached up past Emma's fulsome bosom to

pat her cheek and say, "Emma, mind ye say me to Lyddie, that newest little mother among us. . ." But before she finished her message for Lyddie, Morna broke out singing the heart-rending litany of love for mothers everywhere, "A Mother's Love is a Blessing." At the sound of the old, familiar song, Haim and the others picked up their instruments to accompany the voices that rose in one forlorn threnody beseeching everyone to cherish the blessing of a mother's love while she lives because they'd miss her when she dies.

Now the floor was filled with couples dancing an old-fashioned waltz. The men in their dark clothes, their faces ruddy and shiny, swung the women around until their full-skirted challis dresses swirled out over their boot tops to show the ruffled petticoats beneath. The hall was filled with moving bodies, the sounds of the music and the pounding and shuffling of rubber boots. A blue haze of tobacco smoke drifted over the smells of warm bodies, beer and briney pickled pigs' feet, a delicacy trotted over at regular intervals to the musicians.

One young mother left a fast reel to relieve her heavy breasts which were leaking out their milk. She awakened her baby, who looked around confused at being disturbed. Other babies slept on in the arms of their grandmothers, aunts or neighbours. For a baby one pair of warm, loving arms was as good as another, and caring for the young was everyone's concern.

Hannah "read" a few palms and tea cups, making merry comments here and there. She was sitting alone, cautiously sipping her beer, when someone came up behind her and covered her eyes with a pair of coarse hands.

"That has to be Ben Brack," she said, quickly peeling his hands away from her face.

"You're smart enough tonight, Hannah Holt!" he said, sitting down across from her.

"Just an innocent bachelor until he goes to St. John's," the men liked to say of Ben, nudging and chaffing each other. In World War II Ben had served in the Royal Navy, an experience that had made him somewhat more urbane than his coastal cousins. He even banked his money in St. John's where he visited from time to time, to see his dentist, attend to his affairs — and enjoy a few affairs of another kind. He liked to boast to the men of his chambering and escapades and they enjoyed a sense of vicarious lechery. He was the village gadfly and in some ways maybe a bit of a bounder.

"No palm reading for me tonight, Hannah, but I want a dance — right after the speeches and my slide show," Brack said as he laid a couple of bills in Hannah's bowl and stood up. Stroking his St. John's haircut back conceitedly with one hand, he leaned down close to Hannah.

"By the way, sweetheart, didn't I see your name and the name of the good doctor drawn in the snow just outside the tilt one day when I went down that way? You remember, it was the day I met you and Dr. John on the trail. Did you just happen to spend the night in that tilt with the good man? You don't have to tell me now. I'll see you later for my dance, my maid. I'll be back." And he turned on his half-Wellington boots, looking over his shoulder at Hannah with a wink and a leering grin.

Hannah felt hot anger rising up her neck in a reddening rush. Then just as quickly she refused to be hostess to his inebriated insolence. She pictured her wrath as a little red leaf floating away on a river. It was a river that coursed through her being, carrying off her harassments, making room for an inflow of happiness. With her anger resolved, Hannah made up her mind she would deal with Ben later, face to face, in the dance he would surely come back to collect.

Chapter Sixteen

As though on cue from an invisible master of ceremonies, the dance music stopped and the speeches began. Often the narrator made up his speech as he went along. Serious topics were dealt with humorously while amusing incidents were described in mock earnestness.

Hannah watched Will Speke standing beside Daniel, chafing for his chance to get up on the platform and speak.

Will was a natural raconteur, having started as a little boy to "say a piece" and having come to know the heady intoxication of holding an audience in his sway. He strode forward eagerly, his pleasure shining in his sensitive face. At first Will spoke seriously about confederation, the good points and the less desirable aspects of becoming the tenth province in the Dominion of Canada. The audience listened raptly as he predicted that union with mainland Canada could come about within the year. And then he asked his audience a question.

"Can anyone tell me how you would go about making a man from the mainland laugh when he's old?" There was a low rumble as the audience shifted gears from serious thought to levity.

"Tell us, Will. You tell us!" came the response.

"Well, it's really quite simple. All you have to do is tell him a funny story when he's young!"

Bucked by Will's triumph, Daniel strode over to the platform to take his turn, borne along in the wake of Will's success. He stood up straight and tall as Hannah had taught him to, his hands behind his back clasping each other for courage. Haim's and Hannah's eyes met across the crowded hall.

"Will here has just reminded me of another mainlander joke," Daniel began. "Seems there were two men out here from Toronto a while back and they found a wonderful place for fishing down by the Big Steady. Well, now, the fishing was so good, one of the Toronto men wanted to make sure they could allus get back to the very same spot where he hauled in the big ones. So what d'ye suppose he did?"

There was a rumbling of rubber boots and a murmuring of voices throughout the hall. Then someone shouted, "You tell us, Dan'l. You tell us!"

"Well, now, didn't he take his pen, lean over the side of his boat and make a big X mark on the gunwale! Now he was sure he could get back to the same good fishing spot every day!"

Daniel laughed with his audience and waved his hands in the air when the men shouted up to him, "You can tell them, Dan'l. True enough, boy!"

And then Daniel called out, "But there's more. See, the second Toronto man said to the first, 'That won't work, you dummy, 'cause we may not have the same boat every day!' "

Goaded on by the roar of the revellers, Daniel decided to tell some old folkloric tales he had heard. He described an earlier Newfoundland winter which was so cold that when a woman milked her goat into her dress, the milk stayed frozen until she carried it into the house.

"That same winter 'twas so cold that a man froze his fingers carrying a hot iron he was borrowing from his neighbour's house to press his pants! 'Twas so cold and everyone was so pore that more'n one family et bow-wow stew!" Then Daniel made his way back to Will's side amid more whistles and good-natured pats on his back. The kindly Cove was a good place for gaining youthful confidence.

While Daniel was telling his stories, Ben Brack had been hanging an old square of white sailcloth across one wall. On a cue from Ben, the men turned down the lanterns until the hall was almost in total darkness. With an old battery-powered "magic lantern" into which Daniel fed large, glass-mounted slides, Ben projected black-and-white photos he had taken during his service in the Royal Navy.

A hush fell over the crowd as Ben showed and spoke about what he had seen in the ports of the British Isles, Malta, Sicily, Italy, France, as well as the port of St. John's. No one in the audience minded that a small brown patch in the sail conferred a darkly pigmented blemish upon every face, every ship and every scene in far-off lands, so enchanted were they with their first sight of the terrain of foreign countries with palm trees and soft, sandy beaches.

Hannah could hardly wait to have a dance with Ben so that she might settle with him about his incriminatory comment concerning John and her in the tilt. At that moment Ben was showing a picture of a beautiful young woman he had met in Montreal. Just as Hannah was amused at seeing the patch on the sail look like a large mole on the woman's forehead, she suddenly felt compelled to look out from behind her place by the pillar.

There, his head framed in the window of the main door, was John. How on earth had he managed to get down through the fog? Hannah wondered. She was glad the lights were low, for she thought that the warm feelings rushing through her would surely create an incandescent glow around her.

Hannah saw that John was laughing now. Was he amused

by Ben's pictures? Or was he perhaps laughing at her fellow Newfoundlanders? To whom was he talking every time he turned away and then looked back at Ben's pictures?

Hannah was glad to be seated behind a pillar, where she could peek out and observe John's eyes scanning the crowd without being seen herself. She studied his face with its strong features, its alertness and intensity. Then she saw his face fade, to be replaced by a woman's pale complexion, framed by a nimbus of dark hair — looking like a Spanish princess.

As she studied the face of the beautiful young English nurse, Joanna, whom Hannah knew often travelled with John and sometimes gave anaesthetics for him, the sheet lightning of jealousy shimmered through her brain and her body. But then, Hannah knew she really had no right to have such feelings. Joanna, who was less amused by the scene than John, soon left the window, to be replaced by the dark good looks of Andrew, a Harvard medical student who was studying with John.

Hannah's thoughts tossed like leaves in a wind. Was her intense preoccupation with John a mutual experience between them? Was she alone in discovering that the less she saw of him the more incessantly she thought of him? Hers was surely the same yearning that Anna Karenina felt for Count Vronsky, that Héloïse felt for Abélard. She suspected that such a questing and hungering must be one of the most poignant forms of psychic pain in the handbook of human suffering. And then her thoughts turned instinctively to Haim.

With his slide show over, Ben stared at Hannah until he caught her eye. He nodded and started walking across the room, now filling up again with the dancers.

Ben had as sure a sense of rhythm as did Hannah, and as they danced she felt the sensual undulating gyrations of the gypsy that awaits within every woman for a chance to dance. At first they danced in silence and then Ben studied Hannah's face with a look that quickened something at the base of her spine.

"Do ye remember that morning back last January when I met you and Dr. Weatherton on the trail? The day the priest had been et by the dogs?"

How could Hannah have forgotten? Brack had already told her he had seen their names in the snow. She knew Ben had not said a word to anyone else or she would have been questioned. But Ben had had just enough to drink to make him brazen and garrulous.

"Yes?" Hannah replied cautiously.

"I figure you and the good doctor must have spent the night in the tilt together!"

Hannah knew she had only this moment to set the record straight in Brack's mind. She looked him squarely in the eye, while her feet never missed a beat of the music.

"How dare you talk to me like that, Ben! Dr. John came to help me deliver Angie Prynn's baby down the coast at Abel's Eye. We left there in the afternoon, but we were caught in the storm. Had to stay in the tilt until it cleared. Nothing whatsoever went on between us. What's more, Ben Brack, Dr. Weatherton is a perfect gentleman — unlike you!"

He turned his face to one side and tauntingly looked at her. "'Tis a likely story, Hannah. A likely story. . ."

"It's the truth, Ben."

The music stopped and Hannah excused herself and wheeled around to go back to her table. But just as she did so, she tripped over someone's foot. To her surprise, it was John; and if he had not caught her, she would have fallen. Hannah again felt the gentle flow of kindness she always knew when she was near him. She felt as though she were once more on the swinging bridge of her childhood, as though her feet were not quite touching the floor. She wanted to laugh with relief for she knew from the softness around John's eyes that he felt the same as she did.

At that moment she became aware that Ben was still beside her.

"I'd like another dance, Hannah. . .and to finish our little chat." Ben squeezed Hannah's arm, all the while staring at John, watching his reaction.

Hannah was restless to leave the lecherous, ogling Ben. She was relieved when John freed her from Ben's grip and then engaged him in amiable conversation.

Hannah excused herself from the two men and went back to her table. John soon joined her and sat with his palms outstretched, as though wanting to have his fortune told.

"How ever did you get down here through that fog?"

"I was looking everywhere for you, wondering if *you* hadn't made it through the fog," John said jokingly. "The three of us — Joanna, Andrew and I — came down with the Ranger. Being a seasoned police officer, he knows his way around ice and fog — and he has the right boat for it. The Ranger brought with him a court injunction forcing Ky Henson to go to hospital. We've got him aboard the boat now. He's comfortable enough and we're going to take him back tonight. But there's a bit of a problem. Joanna's had the flu all week. She insisted on coming down tonight because she said she was bushed and had to get out of the Bight. She was sick to her stomach outside just now and Haim saw her. He kindly offered to have her stay in your home for the night. Andrew's going to stay with her. They're engaged, you know."

Hannah was surprised at the relief she felt on learning of the engagement. The blood pulse pounded so hard in her ears that she was not actually certain whether she was hearing a ship's distress signal or not.

John gazed at Hannah, then resting both arms on her table, he leaned forward to look at her more closely.

"What have you been doing to yourself? You've lost

weight, haven't you? You should have an X-ray, Hannah. But tell me what happened to your hands."

"Oh, I just had a tumble over the edge of the Point this morning," she said lightly. "I'd just delivered Lyddie Speke's baby and decided to walk out to the Point to watch the sunrise. Somehow my foot slipped and over I went. But I landed on a ledge just below the peak and managed to swing myself up again!"

John shook his head in disbelief. "I can't imagine anyone surviving a fall from that high Point."

Hannah was almost certain she heard an SOS signal. She looked in the direction of the signal, as though by focussing her eyes she would hear more clearly.

"Listen, John. I think there's a ship in distress. I hope they're aware of two big icebergs I saw out there this morning."

John listened through the music and the laughter of the night and beyond the island of quiet that surrounded the two of them.

"I think you're right, Hannah. Let's go outside and listen."

Out in the night air they heard the distress signal clearly and realized it was coming more often.

"Hannah," John said, "we've got to see about getting out to that ship, wherever it is. I don't think I want the Ranger to go out there. Not with Ky already aboard. And I don't want to take him off the boat now that we've finally got him on his way to hospital. But somebody out there needs help."

"Noah Speke's the man to go with you," Hannah said quickly. "He can smell ice and his boat's got a stretch of canvas up in the cuddy if someone needs shelter. I'll come too because I know where the two big icebergs are — the ones I saw this morning."

John went off to find Noah, while Hannah went looking

for Haim. She nearly tripped over two red-faced boys sitting on the floor beside a barrel of beer. They giggled and poked each other when they were not running their fingers up the seams of the barrel and then eagerly licking them.

"'Tis peasing right through the barrel, the beer is," one of them said, looking up at Hannah with a rosy, cherubic face.

"Peasing right out," the other little boy echoed up at Hannah.

Hannah set the young lads up on their feet and sent them on their way. "Be off with you now, you scallywags. Be off before ye make yourselves sick!"

Haim was used to Hannah's departures out into the night, and somewhat softened by the music and the beer, he merely cautioned her to have a care and to come back first chance.

Chapter Seventeen

Hannah hurried through the fog on her way to the wharf, listening to the ominous orchestration of signal sounds out at the Point, the foghorn playing its tuba to the ship's French horn. In times of crisis at sea, such as this, the lighthouse-keeper changed from the automatically controlled interval of his foghorn's blast and took over its control himself so that he could sound the horn at will in response to the ship's horn. Away from the lamps of the hall the path grew darker at every step until she approached the wharf where the lights from the Ranger's boat, riding at anchor, lent a glow to Noah's smaller boat as well.

At the sound of her quick, light footstep on the wooden wharf, Sergeant Allan Corby, the local Ranger, stepped out onto the deck of the government boat he plied through the northern waters.

Hannah called good evening to the tall, thin officer, who was dressed in a khaki uniform with breeches and high-cut leather boots. But Corby did not respond.

Hannah knew that the Ranger had a reputation for being moody. She wondered if his sullen stance helped him to settle the occasional village brawl; to escort someone criminally insane from the bosom of a quiet hamlet to an institution in the South; or to accompany an infectious tuberculous patient to the hospital in the Bight.

The Ranger shoved his officer's forage cap back on his head, then plunged his hands into his pockets. He cleared his voice to let Hannah know he saw her.

"Oh, good evening, Mrs. Holt," he said peevishly. "Seems like I won't be taking you and the doctor out there in my boat."

"That's all right," replied Hannah, realizing that John must have discussed the matter with the Ranger. "We probably won't be out there long anyway."

Sergeant Corby, who had grown up in St. John's, had gone to sea at an early age and had then returned to study in the constabulary training school in St. John's to become a Newfoundland Ranger, a type of policeman. To mainlanders, the Rangers were comparable to the Royal Canadian Mounted Police on the mainland. And some of their duties were similar. But the Newfoundland Ranger was not only part of the island's constabulary force, responsible for keeping law and order in the outports, he also had to see that the dole was justly distributed.

Noah's open boat, with John aboard, was ready to go. John stretched out a hand to Hannah to help her aboard and Noah started up the faithful old engine. As he steered his boat into the harbour, the Ranger stood on the bow of his ship staring at them through the fog.

Out of the Ranger's earshot Hannah remarked, "Something seems to be bothering Sergeant Corby tonight."

"You're right," John said, sitting down on the gunwale beside her. "We had a discussion about who should go out to answer the SOS. He was determined to go because he felt duty-bound. But I wanted his boat back at a safe base — and with poor Ky Henson spared further confusion. I'm convinced there's someone sick aboard the ship out here."

"I understand," Hannah said, studying his tanned cheeks and the way he sat with one leg across the other, the foot resting defiantly on his knee.

The ship's SOS signal came again, this time closer. During the foghorn's boom-bawn response, John said, "I've missed you so very much since last January and all that happened during that wonderful period of twenty-four hours. It's been a long three months, not seeing you."

Against the hoarse alto of the ship's horn and Noah's harsh whistle, Hannah said, "Nothing's been the same in my life either, John. Nothing."

Then John said simply, "We fell in love with each other. It's almost as though you and I have been in love for a long time."

He squeezed Hannah's hand and they rose to their feet for they were moving beyond the mouth of the harbour and closer to the distressed ship.

As Hannah peered out into the thick fog, she felt again the glow of inner strength she had drawn unto herself that morning as she stood stranded on the rocky ledge. It was as though a fearlessness now lived on within her. As she kept a lookout for the icebergs, she knew that on that day the old constraining membrane under which she had lived for so long had thinned out to the clarity of a bubble, bathed with the iridescence of a beautiful rainbow.

Hannah stepped up behind Noah, who was at the helm. "I think we must be getting close to where the iceberg split this morning, Noah. Just off there a bit to the right."

Noah nodded knowingly. He was wearing his peak cap backward as though to see more clearly into the night. A hand-rolled cigarette hung from the corner of his mouth. He took in two long, noisy breaths. "I can smell the h'ice, sure, Hannah. 'Tis just over there to starboard." His cigarette bobbed up and down as he spoke, its red tip describing an erratic and eerie graph against the dark night.

Noah blew his whistle again and this time the ship responded to it instead of to the foghorn. He slowed the boat down and now it tossed wildly from side to side and up and down like a little shell on the waves of the open sea. The further they moved away from the Cove's harbour and out to sea, the more the sounds of the ship's horn and the foghorn seemed to switch directions, as though they echoed off the high fiordic cliffs around the Point. Then Noah turned off the engine.

John moved nearer to him, trying to see through the fisherman's seasoned eyes.

"We've got to be close to the ship now, Noah."

"Sure, we must. But look, 'tis dark enough to blind a body."

Hannah struggled to settle her surging stomach by looking for some familiar landmark. She was determined not to be seasick. She continued to peer out into the foggy darkness and gradually made out the ghostly forms of the two icebergs.

"Look now, there are the icebergs!" she called out. "Right over there. Hard against the Point. Barely moved since this morning!"

John stared silently in the direction of Hannah's gaze. He shook his head.

"Hannah, you've got better eyes than I have."

"Just look off to one side and let the shapes come to you," Hannah advised. Quite without warning, Noah started up his boat again and John and Hannah were pitched against each other.

"Hold on back there," Noah called innocently. "We're going on out a bit farther."

Now the boat was being tossed wildly about by the waves and Hannah sat down to keep her balance. She took in deep breaths in the hope of avoiding being seasick. She wondered if either John or Noah felt as wretched as she did. But she didn't have long to wonder, for the next moment Noah hung over the side of the boat and "fed the gulls."

John sprang to his side, keeping one hand on the tiller.

"Better sit down a minute, Noah."

"'Tis nothing, Dr. John. 'Twas a pity to lose me cigarette, though," he said with a chortle. "But at least I didn't lose me teeth!"

The ship's horn blew again. This time its direction was clearer for they were away from the confusing echoes in the harbour. Now all three of them felt a sense of their precarious situation as they tossed in the little boat.

John stood beside Noah as he took the boat out a daring distance. Then Noah turned the engine off again, and soon they heard the sound of boot-clad feet running on a metal deck and foreign voices.

Out of the fog they saw the enormous white sweep of a ship's hull looming before them.

"Listen, they're speaking in French," John said.

Someone from the ship's bridge shouted down to them. *"Notre capitaine, il est très malade depuis trois jours. Y a-t-il un hôpital près d'ici? Moi, je suis le sous chef."*

In a mixture of French and English, John told the First Mate that he was a doctor and that if they would lower a ladder he would come aboard and examine the Captain. Within seconds a rope ladder with wooden slats clattered down against the hull of the ship. Noah stood beside Hannah as they anxiously watched John climb up the swinging ladder.

"Isn't that some sight now? Seeing that big ship out here. Have ye ever seen anything the like of this night, Hannie?" Noah was pleased to have been the Captain of the little boat that found the big one.

"I've seen plenty of ships from the Point," Hannah said, as filled with wonder as Noah, "but not up close at sea like this. 'Tis a marvel that you ever found it in the fog and the darkness, Noah."

Meanwhile, John was taken quickly to the Captain's quarters, where he was told the Captain's name was Jacques

Gagnon, that he was about forty years old and that he was from Marseilles.

From the brief medical history John obtained from the Captain's fellow officers and a quick examination, he concluded that the diagnosis was a perforated ulcer. He explained to the distraught First Mate that he would take the Captain to a hospital up the coast aboard a government boat but that they would first have to transport him to the harbour in a fisherman's open boat.

"We'll keep him on his mattress and lower him over the side in one of your lifeboats," John explained in his broken French.

It was only minutes before a lifeboat bearing the Captain was lowered alongside Noah's boat.

"It looks like a perforated peptic ulcer," John told Hannah. "His stomach's as hard as a board: peritonitis. I'll operate tonight."

"I'll go with you," Hannah said. "I'll help with Ky and give the anaesthetic for the Captain."

The delirious Captain lifted a hand as though groping for another hand to hold. In a desperate, operatic cry, he called out, *"Ma chérie, ma chérie!"*

Hannah crouched beside the man and tenderly took his hand in hers. He looked up at her with belcaguered eyes. Beads of perspiration formed on his brow and rolled down the side of his cheeks and into the dark hair framing his ashen face.

The fog had begun to lift. Filled with a sense of urgency, Noah took his boat back into the harbour and pulled alongside the Ranger's boat tied up at the wharf. Hannah jumped aboard the government boat and from there up onto the wharf. She fuelled her lungs with the cool air and ran on up to the community hall.

The moment Haim saw Hannah he hurried from the platform. As he walked toward her through the haze of blue smoke, Hannah noticed that the crowd had thinned. It was almost midnight. The couples with young children had gone home, and so had the elderly. The hardy souls danced on, bent on spending themselves on pleasure before they became bent with age.

"How did Ma get on with the evening?" Hannah asked.

"Dan'l and Will carried her home in her chair and Emma's gone to put her into bed. She had the finest kind of time tonight! Daniel and Will came back and took Joanna, the nurse who's sick, and a student doctor called Andrew up to the house to spend the night."

"Haim," Hannah said, "as Joanna's sick, I have to go north to the Bight with Dr. John tonight on the Ranger's boat. I'm to give the anaesthetic for the sick Captain from the ship that was sending the SOS."

"Do what ye have to, my maiden. But mind ye take better care of yourself than ye did this morning."

Hannah squeezed Haim's arm and turned to go. Near the door a group of fishermen stood in a ring, their arms around each other's shoulders, lustily singing "Ode to Newfoundland." Hannah joined in with the last line — "God guard thee Newfoundland" — as she walked out into the night.

Near the wharf the Ranger came out of the fog. He gave Hannah a quick nod. He held a cigarette with the lighted end turned in toward his palm. Throwing it into the water, he reached out to help Hannah aboard.

"Is Dr. John here?" she asked.

"Oh, he's around here somewhere, I expect," the Ranger said and went to take his boat out of the harbour.

Hannah found John down below in a small cabin with the Captain bunked down on one side and Ky Henson on the other.

With a stethoscope in his ears, he knelt in the space between the two bunks, taking the Captain's blood pressure. He nodded his head rhythmically to the pulse.

As John released the blood pressure cuff, the Captain called out deliriously, "Juan-les-Pins, Juan-les-Pins!" In the chill of the northern waters, he was summoning a warm seaside town back home on the French Riviera.

Hannah spoke to Ky, who lay looking around the cabin in confusion. His coat was unbuttoned, as was his shirt and undervest, exposing his wasted chest. Every time he gave his slow blink, Hannah noticed the round, poached-egg look in his eyes. With his loss of weight, his eyeballs had sunk into their sockets. Hannah fastened his buttons, covering his body against the cold.

"'Tis the right thing to be doing, Hannah," Ky said wearily and smiled up at her. "This business of going to hospital. And I have to remember to thank God for this time of trial, this trouble I've got." Feebly Ky lifted one arm through the air, as he did on the Sabbaths when he preached of the evils of drink, the wickedness in the world and the fires of Hell. He was resigned now, accepting whatever he might have to go through either to regain his health or prepare to meet his Maker.

Once they were out of the Cove and away from the icebergs, the Ranger made good time and they glided into the Bight at half-past two in the morning. The Ranger sounded his horn in a special staccato code which alerted the night watchman to have the hospital truck ready at the wharf.

"We've got to get in and out quickly," John said as they reached the hospital. Hannah, her burgundy skirt flaring out below her navy pea jacket, stood with Ky, holding the door open while John and the Ranger carried the Captain into the hospital.

Hannah felt a rush of love sweep through her as John passed close to her, his body brushing her as he carried his patient toward relief. The little party swept quickly down the main corridor, the same corridor down which Haim had run fourteen years earlier when Hannah was hemorrhaging prior to Daniel's birth.

Hannah and Ky headed for the TB ward while the Captain was carried to the operating room. Before the two parties were out of each other's sight, Hannah was drawn to turn around. In the same instant John looked back and their eyes met.

The traditional TB ward of the time was one long room with twenty beds lined up on each side. As Hannah guided Ky toward the nurse's desk, she smelled the sweet, decaying odour she knew fifteen years earlier when Haim was ill with tuberculosis on the same ward. Most of the patients were asleep, but one or two, awakened by paroxysms of night coughing, gazed emptily into the shadows, waiting for the dawn. Now and then one of them reached out to the bedside table, groping for the square tin which held a waxed sputum cup.

Hannah remembered the nights when one patient's incessant coughing would awaken another until the entire ward was a cacophony of coughing. She became so conscious of the varying stages of the dreaded tuberculosis that she could almost sense who was likely to become a victim.

Its victims, Hannah believed, were labelled with a certain look. It was often nothing more than a vague gaze, haunted and wan. Then came the flush of a sometimes bewildering anger — the kind of ire that some tubercular poets, artists, writers and musicians have known how to exploit in order to leave a creative gift for the world.

Hannah saw that the only nurse on duty was busy with a patient in an end room — a room reserved for the critically or terminally ill. So she helped Ky into a clean, white gown, which lent him the air of a priest in his surplice. Hannah put her arms around Ky's thin shoulders and told him she would see him in the morning. As she left the ward, Hannah looked back at him stroking his long, grey beard like a thoughtful prophet.

When Hannah arrived in the operating room, John had already started an intravenous infusion of saline. One of the hospital orderlies had the same blood type as the Captain and was making his donation downstairs in a clinic room. Hannah washed her hands, put on a cap, mask and gown, and sat down at the head of the operating table. She turned on the anaesthetic machine while John scrubbed. When the Captain was sufficiently relaxed, Hannah gently slipped a curved metal airway into his pharynx to keep his tongue from falling back and blocking his breathing.

John took his place at the operating table. Hannah sensed his restlessness as he waited until the Captain was anaesthetized. The nurses often said John could pace the floor even while standing still. Now Hannah felt his eyes on her, waiting for her to give the sign that he could begin. Their eyes met circumspectly above their masks and Hannah nodded to indicate he could make the incision.

Hannah had to keep her head down as John made the incision because she felt a wave of nausea rush through her every time she saw the scalpel make its first cut through a patient's skin. The incision blossomed open with yellowish fat, red muscles. A moment later, when John deepened the wound to open the peritoneal cavity, there was a gush of purulent, peritoneal fluid, the telltale sign of peritonitis.

Hannah looked up at John who, masked like a knight in white armour, his lance in hand, had already entered the list, and was ready for the tournament contesting disease and death. She looked at the small, gold-rimmed glasses he wore for operating. As he worked intently on saving his patient, John bore no resemblance to the man Hannah had come to know that night in the tilt when he wore no mask and his power was surrendered to tenderness and love.

Quietly the circulating nurse replaced the saline bottle with fresh, warm, life-saving blood while John worked on in silence. But the operating room was not without noise, for the sounds of instruments and machinery created a surgical symphony all their own. From time to time there was the sound of the suction machine sucking up the peritoneal fluids as well as the stomach contents that had leaked out through the base of the ulcer. There was also the heavy breathing of the anaesthetic machine, a sound that reminded Hannah of newly formed, drifting ice being brushed together by a restless sea. Then from time to time the electrocautery machine hissed like a snake as it sealed off a bleeding vessel.

More than an hour had passed when John closed the wound, peeled the gloves from his hands and the mask from his face. He took off the little gold glasses and rubbed the itchy pad marks on either side of his nose.

"Now we'll put him on antibiotics, keep on with the intravenous and keep the gastric tube in place. Lots of deep breathing. Plenty of turning. The next few days will tell the tale. Put him on the critically ill list," John said to the nurses while he and Hannah gently moved the unconscious Captain into a warm bed.

Hannah went into the staff room where she splashed cold water on her weary face. Apart from a brief nap the afternoon before, she had not been to bed for forty-eight hours. She went into the kitchen to make coffee. As she entered John's office, she was delighted to see that he had moved his chair out from behind his desk to be alongside hers and had turned them toward the sun that was beginning to rise over the Atlantic Ocean to brighten the Bight once again.

"It's too beautiful a sunrise not to share it," John said as he sat down beside Hannah. For a moment there was that drift of silence that always followed their being together.

"You must be tired, Hannah. What would you think of spending a few days up here? You could get caught up on some rest and reading. You could see all your old friends — and you've got quite a few around here. And while you're here, you could have an X-ray. You're exposed to a lot of tuberculosis on the coast and, quite frankly, I'm concerned about you. Would you stay here for a week or so?"

Hannah smiled warmly but shook her head. She set her coffee cup down, letting it hit the saucer harder than she meant it to.

"I appreciate your concern, John, but I'm quite sure I don't have TB. I've had a few hard months. Lots of sickness in the Cove. And I've been worried about Ma. I've also been wondering what's going to be best for Daniel. I'm thinking of taking him to Montreal this fall to see about a suitable school. Thanks, I'm touched by your kindness, but I'm leaving with the Ranger at eight this morning. He's going past the Cove, and I have to get back to the family."

John turned a weary, loving smile on Hannah. He reached out and held her hands in his. He kissed each of them in turn, as though to make their scrapes and cuts heal more quickly.

"You can tell the Ranger you're not going back just now. A few days of rest would do you a world of good!"

Despite her fatigue, Hannah felt alive, full of energy and ideas, just as she always did when she was with him. And she knew the loneliness that would engulf her when she left his company to walk down to the wharf. She studied his face intently as though photographing it, to retain it in her memory.

"I have to go back, John."

John smiled enigmatically, leaning forward, his eyes looking into hers. "I understand. But I have an idea. What would you think of having Daniel come up here this summer for a few weeks? We've got a first-rate arts and crafts therapist with us now. She's actually an artist, full of ideas, and has the patients doing all sorts of exciting, creative things. Think about it, Hannah. Daniel could live at the house with Abigail and me. We'd do some travelling together. Maybe even a trip to the Labrador. Daniel would meet people from all over. Who knows, there may even be a craft centre here one day. If the island joins with Canada, there'll be tourists up here, and one day Daniel might be just the person to head up such a centre."

John looked lovingly at Hannah. "I think you know I have great compassion for Daniel. I have had for fourteen years."

The Captain's ship came into the harbour. The horn blew and the Ranger's answered it. Then the Ranger sounded his horn again and Hannah knew the signal was for her.

"Will you look after yourself, Hannah? There's only one you," John said, brushing her hair back. "I think you've got the gold of the sunlight in your hair."

"There's a bit of the moonlight too," she said, referring to the touches of grey appearing at her temples.

He brushed his own hair back. "I guess you'd have to say my hair's almost all moonlight!"

Now they took each other's hands, gazing into each other's eyes as they shared a constrained kiss followed by a hug.

"I'll never forget your offer to help Daniel, John." She brushed her hand over the stubble of his face, hurried to the TB ward to say good-bye to Ky and ran down to the wharf.

Chapter Eighteen

Back in the Cove, Hannah jumped from the Ranger's boat onto the wharf. As she strode toward her home, she thought it was odd that there was no smoke rising from her chimney, especially as Joanna and Andrew would likely still be there.

She was taking off her boots in the outer porch when she sensed an ominous silence. Then she heard eerie, half-crooning, half-sobbing sounds from Daniel, and her heart flooded with anxiety.

Hannah pushed her way through the inner door of her home and right on into the kitchen. She gasped in horror. Her mother lay unconscious on the floor.

Morna was turned on her side. Daniel lay closely along-side her limp body. Hannah watched as he shunted back and forth against his grandmother's body. Then it dawned on her that Daniel was not going to see his beloved Gran'-morna deprived of her soothing rocking chair even in impending death.

Completely unaware of his mother's presence, Daniel raised himself up on one elbow and, crouching over Morna, made the strange sounds — half wailing, half crying — that Hannah had heard outside the door. The boy's tears rolled down his grandmother's pale cheeks.

Andrew and Joanna knelt at Morna's head, taking her pulse and trying to understand what had happened. Despite his late night at the dance, Haim had risen early and gone fishing.

"Daniel, my son, whatever's happened to Ma?" Hannah asked gently as she knelt down beside her moribund mother. But before Daniel could compose himself enough to reply, Andrew offered his crisp diagnosis. "It looks to me, Mrs. Holt, as though your mother has had a massive stroke which rendered her unconscious. It happened about half an hour ago."

Hannah was thankful that at least her mother did not seem to be suffering. She thought about Morna's feisty refusal to have anything to do with tests, X-rays or medication. As Morna lay quietly dying in her daughter's arms as well as those of her grandson, Hannah knew in her heart that this was the way Morna would have wanted to leave for she had dreaded the day when she might have become even more disabled than she was.

Hannah laid one hand on Daniel's flushed cheek and smiled reassuringly at him, tacitly commending him for taking his place by his grandmother's side. It was only a few more minutes until Morna drew her last breath. Andrew and Daniel carried her body into her bedroom. As they laid her gently on the bed, they brushed over a night table, sending Morna's old tin of snuff bouncing down to the floor and sending up a grey cloud that made them sneeze through their tears and even smile wryly that Morna and her box had now both snuffed out.

"It's hard to believe it's Gran'morna, so quiet like this. It won't be the same without her," Daniel said as Andrew discreetly left the room.

Hannah took him in her arms. "She's gone to begin a life free of pain and suffering. We can be thankful for that. And let's be glad for the life she enjoyed. Oh, and didn't she have a good time her last evening on earth?"

For a few moments they stood silently beside Morna's

bed, alone with their thoughts. Then Hannah turned to Daniel. "Would ye mind going next door to tell Noah and Emma? 'Twill be a shock for them too, my son."

Alone in her mother's bedroom, Hannah sat down and composed the telegram she would send to Belle.

In her moment of quiet reflection, her thoughts turned to the Swedish Captain who had fathered her. Hannah tried to imagine what her father would look like as she cast his frame and features from her perception of herself. He would surely be tall, she thought, with fair, greying hair. He would be lean, enthusiastic and. . . Her fantasy came to a halt, for Emma stood in the doorway, one hand to her mouth. Hannah rose and the two women embraced, warming each other with unspoken memories of Morna. Then together Emma and Hannah gave Morna the last loving care the living offer the earthly remains of the dead.

Noah came in long enough to offer his sympathy and to tell Hannah that Will wanted Daniel to stay with him for a while until he had recovered from the shock of his grandmother's death. Noah said he would "make the box" and he set off for the wharf to take his boat down the shore where he knew he would find Haim fishing. It was characteristic of Noah's thoughtfulness that he did not want his neighbour and friend to come home alone to the sudden shock that Morna was dead.

Haim was deeply saddened to find his old friend and ally so suddenly taken from his household. Morna had been more of a friend than a mother-in-law and Haim had always been grateful to her for taking him into her home — when he was convalescing after his surgery for tuberculosis — and where he was welcomed to live both before and after he married Hannah. Haim spent a few moments alone in the room with Morna's body and then he came back into the kitchen where he sat on one of the simple pine chairs.

"I'll say this, Morna had one swing of a time last night,"

he said as though reciting a soliloquy. "'Twas as though she were taking part at her own wake, come to think of it. She even had the last word with death, for she wanted no long dyin'. I can still hear Morna singin' 'Will There Be Stars in My Crown?' I reckon she's got stars in her crown now. . . when ye think of all the people she helped in her long life."

Noah was standing near Haim's chair. His arms were folded over each other and in one hand he held his cap. He was about to speak, but Emma gave him a silencing nod.

Emma stood facing the other three and slowly and seriously said, "I want Morna to have my big store coffin. She's been our queen and she's to have it. And that's that!"

A pall of quiet drifted over the foursome. The coffin had for so long been a forgotten part of the village myth that its very mention came as a shock, especially when it was associated with death.

Hannah smiled compassionately at Emma for she understood her neighbour's need to make a gift of her own materialistic possession. There was perhaps just a hint of false nobility in Emma's voice for she had had many years to remember the misspent money and to shoulder the guilt associated with her misguided purchase.

Hannah knew that the costly coffin would not have impressed Morna in the least. But she also understood Emma's dilemma, and so that afternoon the great mahogany coffin was installed in the Holts' home and Morna was laid down in its tufted, white satin, wearing her best black dress.

Haim took Andrew and Joanna back to the Bight in his boat and dropped off Hannah's telegram to Belle at the post office. Then the three of them called in on Dr. John, who was seeing patients in a clinic. Andrew described the clinical details of Morna's death.

Recalling his own mother's death, John felt a surge of sympathy for Hannah and wondered how she was taking it. Was it only this morning that he and Hannah had watched the sun rise over the harbour from the very same room?

"Come sit down for a minute, Haim," John said, drawing up a chair for the fisherman. It had come to John in a flash that this was a good time to tell him what he had told Hannah just that morning about the possibility of Daniel's coming up to the Bight for the summer.

Haim nodded slowly and a smile crept over his face. He knew how happy Hannah would be to have her boy find a way to do what he loved.

"That might jest work out fine for the boy," Haim said warmly. "And thank ye for thinking of Dan'l. He's a fine lad. 'Twill please his mother too, I'm sure. Hannie thinks a lot about the boy and what he'll do. Maybe she's right that Dan'l shouldn't try to follow in my rubber boots. He's not a bit handy with the sea."

John sensed something new in Haim's attitude toward Daniel. He had expected at least a mention of his being needed for fishing in the height of the season.

"Now I must be off to find the minister to come take Morna's funeral," Haim said.

"Please carry my sympathy to Hannah and Daniel," John said as he walked with Haim to the door. Then he sat down at his desk, and turning his chair toward the window, he watched Haim hurrying down into the town, away from the hospital in which they had both first met Hannah — John a few years earlier than Haim.

Having discussed Morna's funeral arrangements with the local Anglican clergyman, Haim set off for Steadman's Cove.

By the time Haim tied up his boat in the Cove, his house was filled with mourners, some of them reminiscing about Morna. Haim and Hannah heard tales that rounded out the side of the Morna they knew. One of the women, Ellie Spone, recalled the days when Morna helped her look after her daughter Fiona when she was a child deathly ill with diphtheria.

"Morna fair prayed me Fiona back to this world. She prayed and she charmed the sickness away. Y'see, my little Fiona was choking to death, sure. The membrane was over the windpipe and she was dark as night. Morna did something I've never seen before or since. She cut off a lock of me child's hair and carried it with her — next to her heart — when she was looking after Fiona, and then under her pillow the odd moments she napped. 'Keeps it near me halo,' Morna used to say with a little laugh. Whatever she did, she brought that child back to life!"

There were many other testimonials to Morna's kindnesses, her cheer, as well as her cheek and her wit. Ben Brack recalled how one day Morna entertained a circle of folk in the co-op shop, touting the old ways of healing against the newer methods used at the hospital, especially by Dr. John, who she knew was responsible for swaying Hannah away from a faith in herbs and charms.

"There Morna was this day," Ben said, "imitatin' the doctor's New England accent. She was some funny when she said, 'He can't help how he speaks. He's from Boston and all. 'Tis not his fault if he talks like he's got a straw up his nose!' "

Often an amusing anecdote was told over and over until it became part of a family's myth woven right into the fabric of the collective lore of the Cove. Whether the stories about Morna were true or not made no difference to Hannah or Haim. More important to them was the love their friends held in their hearts for Morna.

The day of Morna's funeral Hannah awakened early and went quietly down the ladder-stairs to sit a while beside her mother as she lay in the costly coffin. She lit a lamp and it was then she caught a glimpse of something tucked under the door.

Hannah bent down and drew in an envelope with her name written in jagged letters, the "hand" well disguised.

She opened it and found one hundred dollars. She wondered who it was who wished to remain anonymous. Ben Brack? The Ranger? They were the only two able to make such a gift. Hannah put the empty envelope with her name on it into the fire and resolved to discuss it with Haim that night.

Later that day the minister, Wilbur Coates, came down to the Cove for Morna's funeral and read the steadfast and consoling words from the *Anglican Book of Prayer*. While Hannah played Morna's favourite hymns on the little pump organ, the people sang of salvation and hope.

After the service, Hannah and Emma, the other women and the children went back to the Holts' house to watch the procession of men escorting Morna's body to her place of rest in the cemetery — up by the Point. The great casket gleamed in the brilliant spring sunshine and was a heavier burden than Noah's home-made board coffins ever were for the pallbearers trudging up the great hill.

"There's Haim and Noah," said Emma, straining at the window to distinguish one dark-suited man from another. "And there's Daniel and Will walking just behind them."

When the modest cortège turned one final curve passing out of sight, Emma took Hannah in her arms and the two women wept quietly on each other's shoulders.

It was not so much death that they wept about. The two women wept from a kind of *weltschmerz*, a collective sadness that might have gathered over the months until an occasion, such as Morna's death, could allow unshed tears to flow without question. They may have wept with wonder at the cycles of birth, death and rebirth, a thought possibly triggered by the sight of their sons, now grown to manhood, and taller than either of their fathers. And it was just possible that Emma, dear Emma, may have wept with relief at never again having to play colony to a cumbrous coffin, at being free of the tangible evidence of a frivolous phase of her life long since past.

That night after the remnants of the post-funeral supper were put away and Daniel was sound asleep, Hannah showed the anonymous gift of money to Haim as they sat at a little table. It was not uncommon for someone with the means to leave a gift of money anonymously under the door of a bereaved family, and Haim accepted the gift without the usual questioning that such an incident might have provoked.

"If someone wants to give us summat, Hannie, you and I can accept it with the same lamp, sure," Haim said with a wise nod, not even wondering who might have sent it. Hannah remembered that in earlier days Haim would have been too proud, too independent, to accept anything with the least hint of charity about it, even when it was given in love.

"'Tis an odd enough thing to do," he said, agreeing with Hannah that they would give a tenth of it to buy books for the school. "But if someone feels better for doin' it, 'tis all right by me." Then he slid the money into Hannah's hand.

"Now take it and buy t'ings for the boy and yerself out there in Montreal," he insisted. And when Hannah shoved the money back to him, he said, "Hannie, would ye mind getting me a nice green sweater-coat. I've a like to have one. Not too bright of a green, mind you."

"I was planning all along to get you a sweater, my love," Hannah said. "I might not have thought of a green one but something brighter than your grey, sure."

Haim rested his hands on the table and circled his thumbs one around the other, as he did when he had something to say that mattered to him.

"I saw Dr. John at the hospital — when I took Andrew and Joanna back. Dropped in to see him on my way to visit Ky. He asked me to give you his very best wishes."

Hannah wondered what the two men had discussed.

"Seems like the doctor wants to have Dan'l work up in

the Bight this summer — crafts and such like," Haim said.

Hannah took in a long breath. "The doctor spoke to me about Daniel going north for the summer — the morning I came back from being with the sick Captain, the day before yesterday. I was planning to talk it over with you, but with everything that's happened. . ."

"Well, Han, I'm half come over with relief because the boy's no hand at fishing. Now that we're about to become part o' Canada, Daniel will need summat different to do. I'd be pleased to see him up at the Bight with the doctor, meeting and mixing with people. And, oh, Hannie, I felt tatty sitting there in the doctor's fine office. Maybe 'twas then I decided to have a new sweater — to dizen myself up since you and I might be going up more often to the Bight to see our boy. And, oh, Hannie, isn't that doctor some fine lad of a man?"

Hannah reflected on the two most important men in her life talking together. She felt like a caged bird — with all kinds of domestic seeds close at hand — whose thoughts kept winging away to one ripe sunflower, alone in a field, its seeds packed closely together.

Chapter Nineteen

The days that followed Morna's death were lonely and unnaturally quiet. Hannah, who had grown up knowing only one parent, felt sadly orphaned, like a little boat cut loose from its moorings to set out for the open sea on its own.

But Hannah soon set about brightening up their home. She bought paper and paint for Morna's room and the guest room as well. She would have gone on to paint the whole house, but Haim put his foot down. The smell of paint, he said, made him feel "strange in me chest, like I've no more breath." And so Hannah put away her brushes, happy that for a few weeks, at least, the fresh smell of paint overrode the trenchant odours of cod and dog mash, motorboat fuel and fishnets. But she did wonder just what effect the fumes of the fresh paint might have had on Haim's chest.

Emma had her own personal renaissance after Morna's death, or maybe it was more closely related to the excitement of confederation. It may even have been her being freed of the coffin. She was eager to fill up the space it once occupied with looms and crafts of all kinds.

One day Emma ambled into the Holts' kitchen while Hannah was brushing the crumbs from the stove with an old, white goose wing. She sat down in Morna's well-worn chair and rocked back and forth. Then she looked over at Hannah with her wry neck at an angle ready to pose a question.

"Hannah, my maid, it's been summat strange since Morna's passing. Different altogether. Have you noticed anything a bit out of the way yourself?"

Hannah had felt a sense of freedom and peace about her life.

"Now that you mention it, Emma, something special has been happening. Sometimes it seems as though there are two great wings sweeping my path clear in front of me." She waved the goose wing through the air. "Seems like Morna's always around me, like a mothering angel guiding my days, being all of the things she could not be when she was here with us all. I've not told that to anyone else, Emma. Seems like such an uncanny experience. I've heard tell of such things happening to others, but now I'm knowing it for myself. Have you noticed something the same, Em?"

"Seems like I've burst out doing all kinds of things I've wanted to do for ages — things I did when I was young, sketching and drawing, creating in general. The way I did before I was married. That Daniel of yours has got me stirring up women who'd thought they'd never sew a stitch again. Y'know, I think Daniel's just found out what he wants to do. And now that it looks like the vote for confederation is going through, I'll do everyt'ing I can to help that boy get a shop going somewhere. Sometimes I wonder, Han, just how many sweeps we have left in our brooms."

When the school year ended, Will Speke took Daniel up to the Bight for his summer with Dr. John. They went straight from the wharf to Dr. John's house, where his housekeeper Abigail bade them sit down to steaming hot bowls of chowder. She said they would find the doctor down in the hospital. Daniel left his suitcase in what was to be his home for the summer.

John was still working in the operating room and the boys sat in a waiting room looking at outdated magazines.

But after a while Will left Daniel to keep watch for John while he explored the hospital. Will had often thought he would like to become a doctor, but he had never shared this thought with anyone.

Finally John came out of the operating room and walked down to the waiting room to speak to a little knot of anxious relatives. It was then he spotted Daniel and greeted him warmly.

"It's good to see you, Daniel, my boy. Come along and I'll introduce you to Pamela. She's an artist from England, working with our patients. Did you come up by yourself?"

"No, I came with Will Speke in his boat. But he took off for a walk around the hospital."

The artist was teaching a young woman in a wheelchair how to do crewel stitching. Beside her stood a trolley heaped with crafts.

"Good morning, Pamela," Dr. John said jovially. "I'd like you to meet your summer intern. This is Daniel Holt, a good friend of mine."

John came upon Will in the medical library, where the young man was absorbed in *Gray's Anatomy*. John whistled a few bars of "The Heather on the Hill" from *Brigadoon* until he caught Will's attention. Shaking the boy's hand, he said, "What on earth are you doing in here?"

"I hope you don't mind that I'm using the library?" Will said, then shyly explained that he hoped one day to become a doctor.

After a long chat in John's office, the doctor encouraged Will to apply to medical school at McGill University.

"I'm sure you'll get good marks this last year in high school. I'll write a letter of reference and help in any way I can, including paying your tuition fees."

Will returned bursting with hope for his future. Not finding anyone at home, he went next door to the Holts' house.

"Well, how did you get along at the Bight?" Hannah

asked, seeing a special light in Will's face.

"Daniel's happy as a hare. And I visited Ky Henson, who's coming home soon. Oh yes, and Dr. John asked me to tell you that the Captain's recovered and gone back to France."

Hannah saw that Will had something more to tell her.

"I might be going to medical school next fall," he said brightly. "To McGill in Montreal. Dr. John said he'd even help me out."

Hannah put her arms around Will, then looked proudly into his luminous eyes.

"I didn't even know you wanted to be a doctor. How did you ever keep that a secret, my lad?"

"I've thought about it for years but I didn't want to say anything to anyone until I was sure there was a way for Daniel to do his work too."

* * *

That year the island buzzed with talk of the election. Some were for it, but as many were against it. While Prime Minister Mackenzie King had only a "faltering desire" to bring Newfoundland into confederation with Canada — as the tenth province — the people of the island had their own concerns.

Churchmen feared the effect union would have on the island's denominational system of education — a particular concern for the Church of England. There was also concern about the possible increase in divorce. The merchants in the South feared competition from Canadian carpet-baggers. "Once we're in we'll never get out," they reminded the fishermen of the North. There was a song about the wolfish mouth of the St. Lawrence River about to swallow them all up.

The citizens of St. John's were often described as being "even more British than the British" and were convinced that they had more to lose than did their outport kin.

Many Newfoundlanders hailed Joseph Smallwood as their saviour, a true hero, "the greatest salesman in the world." He campaigned up and down the island, by boat, by plane and by car. His ears often heard the greeting, "God Bless You, Joey!" Many campaign meetings got off to a rousing start with an ear-shattering salvo from a rusty musket. Bonfires were lighted up along the coastal hills. Relatives who had emigrated to the mainland urged the folks back home to support union.

On June 3, 1948, the first referendum for union did not receive a clear majority. On July 22 it went through with a slim win. It was the new Prime Minister Louis St. Laurent who was to conduct the final midwifery delivering Newfoundland into the family of Canada on March 31, 1949. While the outport people hoped for better times, many of the merchants of St. John's were unhappy. On that memorable day there were even black bows placed on some doors. Here and there blinds were drawn down fast. Still others lowered their Union Jacks to half-mast. The island would never be the same, some said in St. John's. And still others told how strong men went off by themselves and wept.

The effects of union were felt almost immediately. Family Allowance brought millions of dollars to the island and the term "baby bonus" became a household word. For many people — whether they were collecting the baby bonus or their Old Age Pension — it was the first steady income they had ever known.

Union with Canada was almost instantly visible in the addition of brighter colours to the wardrobes. The greys and browns and blacks were relieved by bright touches of reds, greens and blues. It was particularly noticeable when the men went down by the water's edge for their Sabbath stroll, for now there might be a yellow sweater-coat peeking out from under a sombre jacket. And then too a few of the women began to join them in their walk, wearing a bright green hat or a new red coat.

Chapter Twenty

It was a beautiful September morning when Haim and the Spekes and many of the villagers went down to the wharf to see Hannah and Daniel off to Montreal. Emma embraced the two travellers warmly at the edge of the wharf and then Haim and Noah took them out in a fishing boat to the coastal steamer that had anchored in the harbour. The two men carried the modest luggage up the wooden ladder. Then they helped Daniel, who put all his courage into climbing up the highly mobile ladder and onto the deck where he beamed with pride.

Hannah was about to make her way up the ladder when Haim handed her a parcel wrapped in newspaper. She looked at him quizzically, suspecting what might be in the parcel from its shape but even more from its smell.

"'Tis a fresh cod for Belle and Delbert. It's been a while since your sister had a bit o' fresh fish." Hannah took the parcel, hoping it would not leak all over her clothes. She put an arm tenderly around Haim and whispered something in his ear. At the top of the ladder, Daniel took the fish from his mother, then helped her up onto the deck.

While Hannah and Daniel were waving good-bye to Haim and Noah, Daniel nudged his mother to look at the sun's reflections on the brass chains Haim wore around his wrists.

"Look at the sunlight on Pa's bracelets!" he said. "Why

does Pa wear those things, Ma?"

Hannah explained that many of the fishermen on the coast wore the brass chains to prevent boils developing on their wrists where the skin had been abraded by the rough edge of their oilskin jackets. "The men believe the bracelets can prevent the water pups — the boils around the wrist — by knocking the head off while it is still only a pimple."

When Daniel and Hannah reached Gander, they gathered Haim's fish and their luggage, then took a taxi to the airport, where they boarded the plane for Montreal.

Hannah and Daniel were not far from Montreal when Daniel became restless, shifting from side to side in the cramped space. He looked over at his mother who was deeply absorbed in *Gone With the Wind*. As she read of life in the old South, Hannah imagined John's wife Cynthia strolling under the magnolia trees, swinging in a hammock, flirting with tall, handsome men on the steps of a white-pillared mansion.

"Ma," Daniel said, "there's something I have to tell you. I've found a friend-girl. Her name is Mary Williams and she's from the Bight. She'd stepped on a rusty nail and Dr. John had to operate. And oh, Ma, can she ever draw something wonderful. She'll have left the Bight by now to go to teachers' college in St. John's. Then she's coming back to the Bight to teach. It's supposed to be a secret, but Dr. John's helping her out."

For a fleeting second the sound of John's name almost took precedence over her son's exciting news.

"Oh and, Ma, she can do anything. And she t'inks I can too! She agrees with Dr. John that a craft shop in the Bight would be good for me. She says she'll even help me. Can't ye jest see me with a customer, Ma? 'Now, Mrs. Patey, and how many of these mats do ye t'ink ye'd like?'"

"Sure, I can see that, Daniel. I know you can do it. And now that we're almost part of mainland Canada, we should know our roots — know who we are, where we came from, what we stand for. One way to keep our past alive is through just what you're doing — creating our local crafts with your hands and teaching others." Then Hannah smiled quizzically at Daniel and said, "My, but you kept the news of your girl friend a deep secret!"

As the pilot announced their descent toward the Dorval airport just outside Montreal, Hannah thought back to the last time Daniel had visited his Aunt Belle and Uncle Delbert. That had been over ten years ago when he was only four. He had reached his manhood in the decade.

"I look forward to meeting Mary one day," Hannah said, realizing that John had probably watched the romance blossom.

They were about to leave the plane when Hannah remembered she had asked the stewardess to put Haim's fish in the refrigerator. With the fish in hand, the mother and son climbed down from the plane into a rush of hot, September air. Hannah knew when she felt the humid air that they were dressed too warmly. Daniel's outfit, which had looked smart when they left the Cove, was now limp and crumpled.

Hannah spotted Belle and Delbert Simpson standing in the meeting area. They were dressed in the light, earthy shades of autumn.

"There's Auntie Belle and Uncle Delbert," she said excitedly.

Belle's dark hair was permed in a mass of curls. She opened her arms to embrace Hannah, then kissed her on each cheek. They were a study in contrasts as they looked into each other's faces: Hannah, tall and fair, Belle, short and dark.

Despite the ten years that had passed since they had seen each other, Hannah and Belle had remained very close. For all her affluence and independence, Belle had never turned her back on Hannah or their mother or on the Cove whence she had sprung. In fact, Belle's sphere of benevolence extended even farther through the educational fund she had established for Newfoundland students from the outports coming to Montreal to study.

"I'm so glad to see you again, Hannie," Belle said, spanning the decade with her enthusiasm. "You're just as beautiful as ever. I can't wait to show you off to my friends. We're having a party for you and Daniel at the end of the week."

As Delbert reached out to take the fish from Hannah, a stream of fluid dribbled down his immaculate trousers.

"Damn it," he said. "This is the first time I've worn these slacks." Then he checked himself. "Never mind." And he dabbed the stain with a brown silk handkerchief.

In that moment Hannah thought he looked like a figure in a wax museum. Or perhaps more like the perfect head of a bird. His black hair, sleeked back to perfection, was relieved only by the white line of the part in the middle. His cheeks were pale and fleshy around his moustache which was tinged with auburn and trimmed and tamed to lie in a thickish mat. He smiled with a roguish air.

They walked out to Delbert's car, a pale-blue Cadillac convertible with white upholstery. He seated Hannah in front, while Belle and Daniel chatted in the back. Hannah smelled the fish and saw that the streak on Delbert's trousers was puckering the fabric.

As they drove along, Hannah realized that there were odours of more than the fish. She knew with a sickening discomfort that she and Daniel had brought with them the indelible odours of home: lamp oil, brine, twine, dog mash and wood smoke. Her uneasiness grew when Delbert turned on an air conditioner full blast, blowing her skirt up around her thighs.

"How does that feel?" he asked, laughing mischievously.

The Simpson mansion in Westmount was just as grand and aloof as Hannah remembered it, with its exquisite panels of Lalique glass in the long French doors leading onto a garden where the flowers were offering their last blaze of colour before winter's gardener would frost them down. Hannah gazed into the long salon, where chairs and love seats were upholstered in either white, mid-blue linen or an exquisite French fabric bearing rich scarlet poppies, purple irises, loosely strewn stalks of yellow wheat and tiny pink straw flowers.

Daniel and Delbert came up the steps with the bags. "My, 'tis some fancy a home," Daniel remarked. Delbert led the way to a guest room adorned with trophies from his seafaring days. There was a sailor's hurricane lamp sitting squatly on its bottom, a ship's compass and a row of sailing trophies. The wheel of the ship on which Delbert had courted Belle was now part of the bed's headboard.

The room Hannah was to occupy was decorated in a maidenly blue, its walls sprigged with bouquets of forget-me-nots and pansies. Hannah was glad to kick off her shoes and feel her feet sinking into the thick carpet of cobalt blue. She wondered how she would put in a week in the flurry of words and noise that was part of the Simpsons' life.

The bathroom in which Hannah had once greeted the dawn of her womanhood was no longer a mushroom pink but decorated with the brilliant blue and green of the sea. The colours reminded Hannah of the view from the Point and she had a brief longing to be back in the heart of the Cove.

From somewhere in the bosom of the great stone mansion there tinkled a tiny, fairy-like bell and Hannah remembered that it was the maid's way of telling them tea was served in the living room. They sat and sipped in awkward silence until Delbert, in a new outfit, sprang to his feet with a burst of energy.

"Daniel, my boy, finish your tea and come downstairs to see my gymnasium. We can toss a ball, lift weights or ride the bikes."

Hannah was troubled but she could not say, Take care of my boy, for he has a problem with his coordination. Instead, she pictured Daniel having fun and began to talk to Belle about their mother. Although Belle had seen little of Morna in recent years, she felt her own kind of grieving. Belle was in England when word of Morna's death reached Montreal — too late for her to attend the funeral.

"Ma was buried in a great mahogany coffin that Emma Speke had bought in a moment of folly and had kept in a spare room until Ma died. It's the finest coffin up in that cemetery!" Hannah said with a shake of her head. "And thanks for sending the gravestone, Belle. It's just. . ." There was a horrendous crash in the gymnasium. Did Daniel drop the weights on his toes? Or on Delbert's toes?

"Don't you want to go down and see what's going on?" Belle asked with concern.

Hannah set her cup down slowly. She had learned long ago not to be a "running mother." And whatever had happened down below was probably less dangerous than what Daniel had often faced in a fisherman's boat on the open sea. The commotion settled down and Hannah told Belle about their mother's last evening on earth when she sang for all she was worth at the dance.

After a while Delbert and Daniel came up from the gym, their faces flushed. Daniel was wide-eyed with wonder at seeing his first bowling alley.

"You should see what's down there right in their house, Ma. There's everyt'ing you could need to get yourself fit. Bikes. Ropes. Weights. Every kind o' t'ing."

"What on earth made that noise?" Belle asked.

"Oh, 'twas just Uncle Delbert dropping a bowling ball."

Delbert went over to the tea tray to pour himself a cup. As he strolled back to his chair, he passed his hand under Belle's chin. It was a gesture that always infuriated her and he knew it. Did he do it to remind Belle of an incipient double chin? Or just to make her angry?

"I expect my little Isabelle will be picking up her Newfie accent again, maybe without even knowing it," he said with a wink at Hannah as he settled himself in a deep white chair.

But Belle was a match for Delbert. "Nothing ever happens around here without everybody knowing it, Del Simpson," Belle said with a demeaning wink as she used a shortened form of his name, which he abhorred.

Hannah and Daniel felt uncomfortable and a little while later they excused themselves to do some unpacking. They were glad to escape what Hannah hoped was only a transient tension in the holiday.

"We've only just arrived, Daniel. The first day's often awkward until a person gets settled in. Tomorrow we're going to do some interesting things. You'll see, it'll get better." Hannah tried to reassure herself as much as Daniel. She remembered once reading that house guests — like fish — begin to smell after three days. Remembering Haim's leaky cod, Hannah smiled to herself that maybe the blight had set in early.

The next day Belle took Hannah and Daniel to look at craft displays, technical schools and artists' supply shops. Daniel was thrilled at the sight of palettes, paints, brushes, as well as the clean, crisp smell of turpentine.

John had paid Daniel for odd jobs around the house during the summer, so while Daniel spent some of his money buying books for Emma, Belle outfitted him with supplies he had never dreamed of owning.

The next day Belle persuaded Hannah to go shopping while Daniel stayed at home with the housekeeper. The two sisters pulled away in Belle's English car, a sea-blue Rover smelling of good leather.

Belle darted in and out among the cars, enjoying a game of wits in the Montreal traffic. As she parked the car, she flourished her hand dramatically. "Hannah, I adore shopping. Now I want to buy you a dress. You're so tall and slim, you can wear clothes beautifully. And you're soon going to be part of Canada. Lots of things can happen. You may not always even be living in the Cove."

Hannah tried to shake off her ennui. But something drew her back to Steadman's Cove with a foreboding unsettledness. And on this golden, mellow September morning, the more she tried to will herself into a happy frame of mind, the more knotted she felt.

When they reached a floor where Hannah was faced with an overwhelming number of dresses, she touched Belle's arm. "Belle, my love, a dress for me has to be simple. It has to be a dress I will wear more than the night of your party. You know how simply we live on the coast."

A tall, blonde saleswoman with a heavy accent rushed forward to greet Belle, who was obviously a regular customer. She brought out dress after dress for Hannah to try on, periodically saying how gorgeous each one looked. But Hannah did not feel gorgeous in any of them. They were about to leave the department when Hannah herself spotted a dress in a rich viola blue.

Hannah fought off feeling like a charity case while Belle made out the cheque and the saleswoman's bracelet of gold charms chimed along with the bell of the cash register.

Away from the dresses Hannah put her arms around Belle and thanked her for the gift.

"It's a dress I feel like me in. I could even wear it in the Cove or up at the Bight. Now there are a few other things to buy before going back to the coast. Could we meet somewhere in an hour or so?"

"Sure, Hannah, but let's not talk about going back yet. You've just arrived."

Having a few minutes of independence restored Hannah's spirits. She found the perfect sweater for Haim, a bright-red woolly hat for Emma, a scarf for Noah, and then she made her way to the book department where she could have spent the rest of the day.

She was looking for a book for John and thinking how

easy it is to find just the right gift for the person one loves. Her eye was drawn to the name Santayana; he was an author she had read with great pleasure. Realizing that the renowned professor had once taught philosophy at Harvard, Hannah took a closer look at the book. When she discovered that it was the most recent volume of Dr. George Santayana's autobiography *Persons and Places*, she bought it, filled with a happy feeling. Hannah concluded her shopping by buying *All the King's Men*, which she hoped Belle and Delbert would enjoy reading as much as she had.

The sisters walked back to the parking lot accompanied by the sounds of car horns, squealing tires and the wail of an ambulance.

"Makes the dog-team trails look pretty simple," Hannah said, huddling close to Belle.

Belle knew how Hannah felt, remembering her own terror at first being exposed to city traffic.

As they entered the driveway, Hannah saw Daniel standing at the gateway to the garden, his sketch pad lying on the grass beside a chair, his face drawn. It was a look Hannah had seen on his face only once before, when he had been out hunting seals with Haim.

"Whatever has happened?"

"Some boys came into the garden and I thought they'd come to visit, the same way we visit back home in the Cove," he told Hannah in the privacy of his room. "But 'twas not like that. Not like anyt'ing I've known before, Ma. They laughed at me sketches. They laughed at me clothes. They made fun of the way I speak. They spoke in English, until they sang a bit of a song in French I t'ink it must have been. Summat about Mankey Poo, Mankey Poo."

Hannah knew enough French to realize that the boys had been chanting *il manque un peu* — he is missing a bit — and she was sick at heart.

Out in the wider world Daniel was like a young deer that had been trained to the gentle ways of the domestic corral and was then set loose where it was a prey to the wolves and wildcats.

Hannah put her arm around Daniel. They sat together while he poured out his troubled heart.

"Listen, my son, people can be stupid and cruel in a way you've never known in the Cove with our own people. But always remember that yours is the way of love. Whenever you come up against someone being unkind to you, don't harden your heart, for then it will have even more pain. Instead, feel your pain, and then let it go. See yourself wrapped in a white cloud of love. Then there'll be enough love for you and for others. Now then, are you going to show me what you did today or am I not to know?"

"It's to be a surprise, Ma. You'll have to wait a while," Daniel said, trying to smile through his sadness.

Chapter Twenty-one

That evening Delbert and Belle went off to a reception. Daniel was still absorbed in his secret artistic task, so Hannah went for a walk. It had rained an hour before and the air was filled with the nostalgic aroma of damp autumn leaves.

As she strolled along the street, Hannah became aware of a teenage boy riding a bicycle, with a brilliantly coloured kite hanging over his back. Then quite suddenly the boy drew his bicycle to a stop beside her.

"Excuse me, ma'am, but do you know the boy who's visiting there?" He pointed to the Simpsons' home.

"Yes," Hannah replied cautiously. "I'm his mother."

The boy scuffed his toe restlessly against the sidewalk.

"Well, this afternoon a bunch of us dropped by to ask what he was drawing out there in the garden. And. . .well, we sort of teased him. Then we sang a stupid song."

Hannah looked at the boy, who stared down at the pavement.

"It was not a nice song. It's called the Mankey Poo. Do you know what it means?"

Hannah nodded her head.

The boy wiped his nose with the back of his hand.

Numbly Hannah watched the boy pass her his kite.

"My parents brought me this from Paris. I'd like your

son to have it."

Hannah looked into the boy's clear blue eyes. "That's very kind of you, son, but Daniel is the person you want to see. Come on into the house and I'll tell him you're here."

Hannah left the two boys to make their peace.

Daniel accepted the apology as well as the gift. Later that evening as he handed the kite to his mother, he said, "'Twas nice of him to come by. And it's a fine enough kite, sure. Some day maybe we'll fly it back at the Cove."

The next day Belle left Hannah with her cherished hairdresser and took off on some errands. It was the first time Hannah had been to a hairdresser's "parlour," as Antoine's emporium was called, and she smiled as one operator after another let her long blonde hair tumble through their fingers. "Where did you ever get hair like that?" they asked her. And Hannah just laughed and said, "You have to live in the Newfoundland fog."

Hannah sat patiently while they set her hair and put her under a hot metal helmet. She tried to read a magazine but was intrigued with watching the other women.

Antoine, wearing rosy glasses, coiled Hannah's hair into a trellis up the back of her head. Hannah thought it looked horribly like the Medusa. The staff had gathered to "ooh" and "aah" just as Belle came in.

"Oh, you look absolutely fabulous, Hannie. Don't you think so, girls?"

Hannah felt like a prize animal trussed up for some kind of fair. She liked her hair best when she felt the wind combing through it high on the Point.

On the way back, Hannah asked Belle if she would stop at McGill University, for she wanted to pick up some brochures about the medical school for Will Speke.

"I'm always happy to go back to my old alma mater.

My years at McGill certainly changed my life," Belle said. "And look, Hannah, if Will comes next year, we'll help him in any way we can. The same goes for Daniel. But, Hannie, what kind of life are you having out there in the Cove?"

"Oh, I'm fine in my own self. And this summer Daniel was up at the Bight where he worked with arts and crafts. It was Dr. John Weatherton's idea. Daniel stayed with the doctor."

"Dr. John Weatherton. I remember him well. Very handsome. Soft Boston accent. He was more than a man, if you know what I mean. He had, as I remember, a strong presence."

To hear Belle speak of John with such admiration almost brought tears to Hannah's eyes.

As the two sisters walked through the hallowed halls of McGill, Hannah pictured the young Will Speke evolving into a doctor. Would he return to the coast as a family doctor or become a fashionable private practitioner in Montreal, or perhaps even a professor?

Back at the Simpsons' mansion, Daniel was keen to see the pictures of the school where Will might be a student. He carried the literature off to his room, beckoning his mother to come with him.

As it turned out, Delbert had come home from his office and taken Daniel shopping for clothes. To Hannah's amazement, Daniel proudly showed off his new wardrobe — slacks and sweaters and shirts and a new pair of shoes.

"The suit'll be ready by tomorrow. On time afore we leave for home, depending on when you're ready to go."

"Would you like to go home soon, my son?"

"Any time when you're through visiting with Auntie Belle, I'm ready to go back. I've had a wonderful chance to see arts and crafts in the stores. And I'm glad to have some new clothes, the kind I can wear in the Bight. Now that we're about to become part of Canada, I've a different feeling for clothes. And if I do go to work in the Bight, 'twill be a different kind of life. Oh and, Ma, I'd like to get back to see if there's a letter from Mary Williams."

With the time for their return settled, Daniel stayed in his room, putting the finishing touches to his surprise. Hannah dismantled the coif rising up the back of her head and combed it to fall over her shoulders.

The next day, in preparation for the party, Hannah and Daniel blew up balloons and wove yellow orchids around pillars and chandeliers. Hannah tried to put herself into a mood for the party.

"Ma," Daniel said, "funny t'ing, I've just remembered a dream about Pa."

"Oh, now, and what did you dream?"

"He was coming back to the wharf. His boat was piled up high with fish. There was no one else around. Then Pa did summat strange. He threw each and every fish back into the sea. Then he tied up his boat and walked back to the house very slowly. But it was clear, Ma, just like I was walking beside him."

The dream only intensified the uneasiness Hannah had been feeling.

"Daniel, we're going back very soon. I'll speak to Delbert in the morning. He'll arrange our flight."

That evening Hannah dressed for the party in her new blue outfit — with its alluring neckline, small waist, full skirt — and Daniel proudly wore his new tweed suit. Belle and Delbert told them they looked magnificent.

The couples began to arrive, making serious work of small talk until the men glided off to the bar. To Hannah's ears, some couples seemed to talk to each other with the politeness of sales clerk and customer. A few lone men came in with a look of quiet expectation. As a beautiful and apparently unattached female, Hannah was never long without an interested male at her side. There was one of Delbert's colleagues, for example, who introduced himself as Clifton.

"I work with Delbert," he said. "He's told me a lot about you, but he didn't tell me all, obviously." His wide eyes roamed down Hannah's slender body. "How come your husband lets a beauty like you out alone in Montreal?"

"My son Daniel is with me. He's right over there," Hannah said proudly.

"He's a fine-looking boy. Looks a little like you."

Just then Delbert slipped his arm around Hannah's waist on his way to change the Harry James record. "Don't believe a word this man says!" he whispered. Then he turned to Clifton. "Are you making passes at my little seaside sister-in-law?" Delbert swept away from Hannah, gathering Belle into his arms, and together they did an exaggerated version of the conversation dance step down one side of the long salon.

Hannah pictured John talking to Clifton, to Belle, to Delbert, thinking how amiably he would move among them and then how genially he would excuse himself from the boredom of it all. She thought too of Haim, of the happy dance that had taken place back in the Cove last spring.

"Speaking of the seaside," Clifton said provocatively, "reminds me of a Newfoundland joke I'm sure you'll enjoy. There was a couple savouring those last moments of sleep just before their alarm was to go off. Suddenly the telephone rang. The husband picked it up. He said 'Hello.' For a few seconds he just listened. Then he burst out, 'How the devil should I know? We live thirty miles from the coast!' And he slammed down the phone.

"'Who on earth was that?' his wife asked.

"'Oh, some stupid idiot! Can you imagine, he wanted to know if the coast was clear!'"

Hannah laughed at his joke but even as she cast her eyes

around the room, planning her escape from Clifton, he leaned forward and whispered in her ear, "Listen, my lovely, how's about you and me having lunch together tomorrow — or better still, dinner? My wife's still up north at the cottage."

"My husband's up north at our cottage too," Hannah said with a distant smile. "And I'm going back to him very shortly. Thank you just the same."

A short, stout woman in a pink silk dress with large sleeves drifting through the air like kites came over to Hannah. "My dear, we're all dying to talk to you. Do come and join our group over here." And she whisked Hannah away to a little circle.

"We've just been talking about our pets," one of the women said. "Do you keep a dog, Hannah?"

"We have about nine or ten dogs most of the time," Hannah said.

"Oh, you must have enormous veterinarian bills then," someone else said.

"Oh, no," Hannah protested. "We don't have animal doctors up where I come from. You see, the husky dogs are actually wild. They live outside in their pens. They're working dogs. They pull the sled when somebody has to go to hospital or they. . ."

"Isn't it in Newfoundland where they have such large families?" interrupted a woman whose thick grey hair was swept back from a pair of equally grey eyes looking out at Hannah over a gold pince-nez.

"Some of the families are quite large," Hannah said, feeling the chill of assessment.

"How many children do you have, my dear?"

"I have one child. That's my boy over there talking to his Aunt Isabelle." Hannah remembered in the nick of time to call Belle by her Montreal name.

"Well, that's quite unusual. How many children would

there be in the largest family in your community?"

"Our lay minister and his wife have had twelve children."

The woman with the pince-nez grimaced and explained that she was the president of the local birth control society. She was horrified to think of any woman raising twelve children. But she was soon caught up in talking to the person on her other side, while her husband chatted with Hannah.

"Myrna does get herself a bit worked up about planned parenthood. I hope she didn't offend you."

Before Hannah could answer, Daniel came over and said he was going to his room to finish his surprise gift for Belle and Delbert. Hannah walked with him to his bedroom, half envying him his freedom to have privacy. She put her arms around Daniel and kissed him good night, thankful that they lived in a village where they could count on the laughter, the love and the tears coming only from the heart.

Hannah picked up a glass of wine and went back to the party, only to find the birth-control lady's husband waiting to resume their conversation. As it turned out, he was once associated with Delbert's father and had on one or two occasions sailed around the shores of Newfoundland. It was, he said, "a pretty barren rock of a place."

"Well, there are some very beautiful scenes along the coast, as well as inland, and the people are warm and wonderful," Hannah said proudly.

When the last guest had finally left, Hannah thanked Belle and Delbert for the party. Since the music was still playing, Delbert swept Hannah off her feet and twirled her around. "You're a beautiful lady and I'm glad to have seen you out here again. I only hope it won't be so long until the next time."

That night Hannah had trouble getting to sleep. She was restless to return to Haim. As her thoughts tumbled about, Hannah recalled a line she thought was written by Blake to the effect that sometimes a person does not know what is enough unless he knows what is more than enough. . . .

The next day Daniel showed his mother a water colour he had done of the Simpsons' home and garden and a sketch of McGill University for Will Speke.

"I've a present for you and Pa too, but I can't show you until we're on the plane."

Two days later Daniel and Hannah took their leave of the Simpsons.

"One day we'll come out and visit you," Belle said. "Not this year. But maybe next. This is for you, my darling Hannah. You're not to open it until you're back home!" And she handed Daniel a large, burgundy-coloured suitcase.

They were airborne only a few minutes when Daniel rummaged in his bag for the gift he had made.

"This is what I made for you and Pa." Proudly he handed over a flat box.

"What's in here?" Hannah asked, looking from Daniel to the box with child-like curiosity. Hannah took the lid off, and there lay a family tree that Daniel had done in water colours.

"See, Ma, I didn't want to show you it at the Simpsons' for they have neither child and they might have felt badly. But look, there's Gran'morna. There's Grandpa Walt. There's you and Pa and Amity and me. And room for more. Maybe Mary Williams' name will be there one day too, Ma. See, I found the idea in a book that Belle gave me. And I t'ink we could embroider family trees to sell in the shop we're going to open one day in the Bight. Folks could take the tree home and stitch in their own names."

As Hannah looked at Daniel's gift, she longed to tell John how much she appreciated his doing what neither she nor Haim could ever have done for their boy. Daniel had matured so rapidly in recent months that Hannah had to ask herself if it was only last spring when he had come home devastated from the seal hunt.

After a rapid flight to Gander, Hannah and Daniel

boarded a steamer which would take them northward to their home.

The evening their ship pulled into the Cove, it was darker than usual because of a rapidly gathering fog. Being a smaller steamer than the one they had gone out on, they were able to disembark right at the wharf. There was no one about that evening as they made their way, laden with heavy luggage, their footsteps sounding hollowly on the wooden boards. To Hannah the evening air seemed unnaturally cool and quiet.

It was perhaps the smell of the fishy air that reminded Daniel of the cod they had carried out to the Simpsons.

"I bet that codfish went right into the garbage the same day Uncle Delbert's pants went to the cleaners!" Daniel said with a hearty laugh. And Hannah agreed.

When they were closer to their house, Hannah observed that there was no smoke rising from the chimney and that the house was in total darkness. She said nothing to Daniel but pressed on more quickly.

Dropping the heavy luggage on the steps, she pushed on into the house. Even in the darkness she could see the kitchen had an ominous tidiness about it.

"Where's Pa?" Daniel asked anxiously.

"I just don't know, Daniel. But let's light a lamp and see what we're doing."

It was Daniel who first spotted the note over by Haim's yellow clock. He read it aloud to his mother:

> *Dear Folks — come on over to the house when*
> *ye're home. Come any hour at all. Love, Emma.*

In the chill of their unheated home, Hannah drew strength from the power she had known on the Point. Now with the Cove bathed in fog and the horn blowing once again, she pictured the colours of the rocks glowing warmly in her mind. She braced herself to walk with Daniel over to Noah and Emma's house.

Chapter Twenty-two

Noah and Emma were seated at the table just finishing their evening meal. At the sight of the two beloved travellers, Emma dropped her fork and ran to take them both in her arms at once.

"Oh, and is it some good to see the pair of you, Hannie and Daniel! But sure aren't you back a few days sooner than you planned to be?"

"Whatever's happened to Haim?" Hannah asked desperately, looking from Emma to Noah.

"Well, my dears, he took a poorly spell two days after ye left. He tried to keep on working. Wouldn't go at all to doctor. But by chance didn't Dr. John drop into the Cove two days later on his way back up to the Bight. He called at your house but Haim was out fishing. Then he called at ours and we were out too. So, according to Twyla Henson, who saw him both coming and going, it seems Dr. John took a walk out to the Point for some reason or other."

Emma was not yet through. "Seems like by the time he got back from the Point, he saw your door ajar and he went in. That's when he found Haim back early from fishing. Too sick from coughing up blood to get up again and go on. Seems like scattertimes the old TB has a like to flare up. Dr. John took him straight to hospital and wanted to send ye a telegram but Haim would not let him. Now

sure'n they can do wonderful t'ings in hospital. . ." Emma
took Hannah in her arms.

As Hannah was to learn later, the day John had found
no one home, he had acted on an impulse to go out to the
Point to see the perilous place where she had watched
many a dawn come up.

On that fateful September morning, John guessed that
Hannah and Daniel were probably in Montreal and that
Haim was out fishing. Driven to make his private pilgrimage along Hannah's accustomed haunts, John was also
hoping to assuage his loneliness and longing, deepened
during the summer by his closeness to Daniel.

It was seldom that John took time to walk for the sheer
pleasure of it, and on that cold September morning, his
hands free of his medical bag, he strode along toward the
Point, the place where he imagined that Hannah's fantasies
gave way to dreams.

John passed the local general co-operative store, with
a scattering of dead flies at the base of a pot of gangly
geraniums and a black cat sleeping in the window. It was in
the Co-op store that the women of the Cove gathered for a
bit of comforting chat, much as the wharf was the rallying
place for the men to gossip, to spit tobacco juice into the
harbour and to tell the truth at least as they interpreted it.

John stopped to look at the frame schoolhouse where
he pictured Hannah as a child: a leggy leaf of a girl with
questing eyes which could just as surely be laughing and
playful.

Soon he came upon the white frame church. He walked
in through the unlocked door and sauntered down the aisle
toward the altar with its plain wooden cross, down to the
spot where Hannah had probably stood as a bride of nineteen. He walked to the fount where Daniel must have been
baptized. To one side of the fount stood the modest brown
pump organ which he pictured Hannah playing every

Sunday. Just as he was about to leave, John turned back and knelt on one of the wooden kneelers. Although he did not consider himself a deeply religious man, John believed in the power of prayer and the existence of the Divine Spirit. Taking a lingering gaze over the holy place, he offered a silent prayer of thanks for his friendship with Hannah.

Close to the top of the Point, John looked out over the ocean, sparkling with the September sunshine. He stood for a moment outside the little cemetery and then he undid the twist of rusty wire and walked in, recognizing here and there the names of patients whom he had comforted through their transitions from this world to the next. He saw Morna's roughly earthed-over grave where the red dye from paper flowers had seeped scarlet over the lumps of clay. At the head of the grave stood a handsome new stone bearing the dates of Morna's birth and death and the words: *She Hath Done What She Could.*

In an older part of the cemetery he found the grave of Amity, bordered with garlands of shells gathered, John assumed, by Hannah's own loving hands. Reflecting on the white concrete baby's hand reaching up to touch the angel's wing, his eyes filled with tears at the grief Hannah had known.

Kneeling at the edge of the Point, John looked down at the life-saving ledge onto which Hannah had fallen back in April of that year and he marvelled at her strength to hoist herself to safety. John rose to his feet, gazed westward toward Montreal, then slowly turned to go back down the hill.

Closer to the Cove, John could see that the Holts' door was now half open. Had Hannah and Daniel come home? Nodding to this person and that one, John anxiously made his way through the village, being detained briefly by Twyla Henson's inquiries about Ky.

John knocked at the Holts' open door, then walked past the rubber boots and outdoor clothes. As he called out, he pushed open the inner door. Haim was slumped in his rocking chair, his face flushed.

"Began to have scatter pains in me chest a few days back," Haim told the doctor. "Thought 'twas the flu. Hannie's gone with the lad to Montreal." Then he started to cough up blood into his handkerchief.

On his way back from the boat with his medical bag, John met Emma, who had run out to hear some word of Haim. "Noah wanted to take him up to the hospital, but he wouldn't go," she said, hurrying along on her short legs and wrapping her arms around herself to keep warm.

"Do you know when Hannah's planning to come back?" John asked.

"Depends on what Dan'l finds out about school. Oh, and Dr. John, thank you for what ye're doing for our boy Will. 'Tis some good to think he might take up doctorin' just like yourself. But I won't keep ye now. I'll come over in a bit to help Haim get ready for I'm sure ye're taking him to hospital."

When John reached the Bight he sent someone for a wheelchair for Haim because he had been seasick during the boat trip and was too weak to walk. As John pushed Haim's chair up to the hospital, the first snowflakes of winter drifted down.

Haim was admitted to the same ward on which Ky Henson was recovering from a thoracoplasty, the same operation on the chest wall that John had done for Haim many years earlier. Ky was shocked to see Haim looking so sick and miserable.

"You'll be better the once, Haim," Ky said. "Look at me now. Took on fifteen pounds since I come up here."

One look at Haim's X-rays confirmed John's suspicions: he had miliary tuberculosis, a widespread dissemination of the disease often called galloping consumption by the people along the coast because of the alarming rate at which it ran down its prey and consumed it. In that era its progress was ruthless and rapid. That same afternoon John finally persuaded Haim to let him send Hannah a telegram urging her to come right home.

As it happened, however, by that time Hannah and Daniel were already on their way back to the Cove. . . .

* * *

Noah rose from the table to join Emma in welcoming the travellers back home again. As he walked toward the two, Noah lifted one of the stove's round lids and sent a spurt of tobacco juice hissing among the flames.

"I'll take ye and Daniel to the Bight in the morning. 'Tis too foggy to set out in my boat tonight."

Just then Will rushed into the house, delighted to see Daniel and Hannah again. Daniel wanted to tell Will all about his visit to Montreal, to give him the sketch of McGill University, but he sensed his mother's wish that he return home with her.

Back home, Hannah turned to Daniel, her eyes flashing with determination. "My son, I'm going up to the Bight tonight. To be with Pa."

"But how will ye go, Ma? Uncle Noah says it's too foggy for a boat. No snow for a team o' dogs."

"I'm going on foot. Up on the trail the dogs use," Hannah said, reaching for her old travelling bag.

"But 'tis all of fourteen miles of gorse and bog. 'Tis slew-footed walking all the way. 'Tis dark and the fog's come on. Are ye sure ye should do it, Ma?"

"I know I should do it, my son," Hannah said with a toss of her head. And she packed an axe, a flashlight, Haim's new sweater, her diary, a bottle of water, some biscuits and a few personal things. Then she remembered to take Haim's clock. As she wound it, holding it in the palm of her hand the way Haim used to, it struck her that Haim had not been himself ever since Morna's death. Had some light gone out of his life with her passing? she wondered.

Hannah hurried up the ladder-stairs to dress in warmer clothes. When she came down, Daniel had changed too, and was holding a lighted lantern to carry on the end of a pole.

Tears filled Hannah's eyes at the sight of Daniel standing by the old kitchen door, ready to take his part on the long, arduous trek to see his father.

"I couldn't see ye going up there alone, Ma. Besides, I want to see Pa too. And d'ye know summat, Ma? I t'ink I've just figured out the meaning of my dream about Pa in Montreal."

Knowing what Daniel was thinking, Hannah put her arms around the boy and held him for one strengthening moment before she remembered to leave a note for Noah who would surely be over in the morning.

A bone-chilling cold wrapped itself around them that foggy September night when they set off on the trail, the same trail the Beothuk Indians once travelled — before they were massacred by the white settlers. But as they slogged through the bog, they were soon warm enough, for they were dressed for the colder weather about to set in. They trudged over the gorse, once in a while exchanging thoughts.

"This is the trail, Daniel, over which your pa drove me by dog team the night you were born. 'Twas a wonderful snowy night with a full moon and Northern Lights everywhere. They played like a rainbow halo over the Bight. And what a fine little laddie of a baby you were, Dan'l."

Soon they were caught up in trying to make their way across a wide watery bog which looked as though it would invite them to sink to their knees in its murky depths. A day or two later the bog would have been frozen. But on this unusual night of fog, another of the fickle, equinoctial turns of weather, Daniel had the added task of balancing the lantern out at the end of the pole while steadying his footing.

It was a comfort to Hannah to know that Haim would be having the best of care, probably from John himself. She shivered at the thought of what might await her at the end of this muddy trail, but she knew she had made the right decision to set out for the Bight that night.

Daniel swung his arm out to stop his mother from walking into what looked like a treacherous bog. "Stay where ye're to, Ma. We'll have to lay down branches to get across."

Hannah held the lantern while Daniel scrounged around for bits of boulder and a few branches to give them a footing over the watery pit. Now that they were more than three-quarters of the way to the Bight, Hannah began to look through the fog for High Rock, the menacing boulder that had caused her fateful spill out of the komatik the night of Daniel's complicated birth.

It was when they stopped to quench their thirst and nibble on biscuits that Hannah saw through the fog that the high spike of granite was just a few feet ahead of them. She took the axe from her bag. "Daniel, my son, for many a year I've wanted to knock off this bit of rock. It's a proper menace to a dog team when it's covered with snow. I'll use this axe to send it flying!"

Hannah dealt one savage blow after another, swinging the blunt end of the axe against the granite spike, until she sent the jagged tip of the boulder flying into the night.

Daniel watched his mother, not realizing that this was the pivotal rock which had catapulted both of them on a dangerous trajectory to land in a bank of snow a few feet away. When Hannah had stowed her axe back in her bag, Daniel shunted the entire rock back and forth until he rolled it completely away from the path.

Daniel brushed one hand against the other, then squared his shoulders. "Figured I might just as well move the whole t'ing away. Never know who might have croppered on it."

They were pleased to have rolled away the stone and they pressed on, feeling their weariness the more for having stopped for a few minutes.

They both started when they heard a swishing sound not far from their path. But they kept on going, trying not to think about the tales they had heard of lynx and wolves in these woods. The rustling grew closer, then seemed to stop and start up again, as though walking along its own parallel path in the woods. Hannah tried to convince herself that it was only a small creature reshaping itself in sleep, but her heart beat faster and faster and her footsteps were slowing down.

"'Tis like as not only a partridge, Ma, wonderin' just how much longer we're going to upset its sleep. 'Tis no time to be nervy now. Just keep on walking." Daniel took his mother by the arm and propelled her along the trail.

Just then something ran close to their path. Hannah's heart felt as though it had stopped beating and was hanging somewhere in the middle of her chest. The noise was closer now and Daniel, while steadying his mother with one arm, suddenly let the lantern slip from the end of the pole. Fortunately, the lantern stood where it fell, still glowing.

As Daniel darted forward to pick up the lantern, something bounded out of the woods. "Ma," he laughed with great relief, "'twas only a hare! Look at. . ."

A huge night bird swooped over their heads. But they scarcely missed a step, such was their state of raw nervelessness.

By five o'clock in the morning, close to six hours after they had left home, Hannah and Daniel reached the hospital, their clothes muddied and their hearts anxious. They pulled off their boots and left them at the door and went into the washrooms to freshen up. Then together they walked down the long dimly lighted corridor to a desk where a nurse was writing on a chart.

Chapter Twenty-three

"Excuse me, nurse, I'm Mrs. Holt and this is my son Daniel. We've come to see Mr. Haim Holt. How is he now?"

"He was very restless earlier on, but he's calmer now. He asked for you many times during the night. I'll take you to his room. He's very ill, Mrs. Holt. Very ill. I'll get you gowns and masks. He has miliary tuberculosis."

"Is Dr. Weatherton in the Bight?" Hannah asked anxiously.

"He's had to go up the coast on a call, but he was here most of last evening. He's been spending a lot of time with your husband. He expected to be back some time this morning."

Except for the moments when one hand plucked erratically at the coverlet, Haim lay quiet and still. Hannah rested her masked cheek against his florid face. His eyes looked up as though he were viewing her from a great distance. His breath smelled like the sweet vapour rising from a pot of boiling rice. Then Haim smiled and nodded slowly and weakly.

"Daniel's here too, Haim," Hannah said, drawing the boy toward his father. Daniel's eyes looked as though he could not believe what he was seeing. Gently he took his father's hand in his, unable to find words for what he wanted to say.

Haim's parched lips drew apart to speak. The one hand

left off plucking the coverlet to rise weakly into the air, then to fall again.

"I knew ye'd come," he whispered. "I called for ye all through the night and ye must have heard me, sure."

It was clear to Hannah now why she had felt compelled to return early from Montreal. Dipping into her bag, she pulled out the new green sweater she had bought for Haim and then held it up for him to see.

"I got this in Montreal for you, Haim dear."

Haim smiled and said huskily, "Put it over me chest, Hannie. Put it over me now."

Hannah laid the sweater across his chest, as though it were a sacerdotal garment and he were a priest garbed for some holy rite. She took Haim tenderly in her arms and held him long and lovingly. When she straightened up, Haim reached out for Daniel.

"Dan'l, me boy, 'twill be fine if'n ye don't go fishin' or sealin'. Ye can do whatever ye want to do," the father whispered through a gravelly voice as he drew Daniel toward him, granting him his blessing for life.

Although familiar with the unblinking eye of death, Daniel looked bewildered and flustered.

Just then Hannah remembered that she had brought Haim's yellow clock and she laid it beside his ear. At the sound of the ticking, Haim smiled and tried to focus his eyes on Hannah. His hands stirred as though he were trying to reach out to her. At this point Hannah and Daniel, one on either side of the bed, each slid an arm around Haim and held him until that moment when his last slow, stuttering breath sucked in the little hollow at the base of his throat.

For a few minutes Hannah held Haim's hands, praying for the journey of his soul to its new life. Then she walked around to Daniel and gently took him in her arms.

They sat quietly by Haim's bed, composing themselves. Then Hannah took Daniel to the waiting room before going back to speak to the night nurse.

"Shall I send a message to Dr. Weatherton?" the nurse asked.

"Thank you, but I'll just go up to his house myself. I'm anxious to know about my husband's last days." With that, Hannah wearily propelled herself toward the waiting room where she saw that Daniel already lay sleeping under a dark-blue blanket.

Hannah washed her face and hands and combed up her hair. Then she remembered she would have to scrub last night's mud from their boots. But when she went out to collect them, she found that the four boots stood spotlessly clean. Somehow the little anonymous act of kindness reached deeply inside Hannah, tapping the vein of her unshed tears. She wept as she pulled on her boots. Drying her eyes, she straightened her spine and started off toward the path that led to John's home.

Hannah knocked on the handsome blue door, staking her hopes on the footsteps coming closer toward her from within the house. But the footsteps, Hannah thought, were too fast for Abigail, and too light to be John's. In her state of exhaustion, Hannah stood speechless at the sight of Cynthia standing before her in a finely woven brown suit with a pink satin blouse.

"Good morning," she said to Hannah in her southern accent. "Won't you all come on inside?"

Hannah's legs felt weaker than they had on the long trek from Steadman's Cove. She struggled to control her emotions. "My name is Hannah Holt. I was just wondering if Dr. Weatherton might happen to be in. You see, it's about my husband. He has just died."

"Oh, I am sorry. Do come in," Cynthia said with warm sincerity. "I think I remember you from the days when you worked at the hospital."

"Yes, that's right, Mrs. Weatherton," Hannah said.

"As for the doctor, I don't rightly know when he'll be back. He's gone out somewhere. Up the coast a way, I think. I was asleep when he went out. But you're welcome to sit down and wait." And Cynthia led the way into the living room. "Do excuse all these packing cases."

When Cynthia waved one hand over the luggage, the light from a lamp fell on her ring, radiating a shaft of blue light sparkling through the room. Hannah traced the dazzling ray to the large sapphire at the heart of the ring; diamonds and pale-blue gems supported the master jewel. The ring was like a magic lamp casting its spell every time Cynthia moved her hand. To Hannah it seemed to be possessed, like a genie's tool of enchantment, and she reached for the door, eager to get out of the house.

As Hannah walked down the path, she steadied her tumbling thoughts by remembering the days when she lay in a hospital bed with the infant Daniel in her arms, watching for a glimpse of John making his way along the same stony trail. Still stunned by Haim's death and the sight of Cynthia, Hannah wondered if the luggage belonged only to Cynthia. Or was it John's too?

Hannah was unaware that John, now walking up from the wharf, was watching every step she took away from his home.

As Hannah hurried back to the hospital, something drew her eyes toward the wharf – that intuitive perception whereby we know when someone special has just entered a crowded room or is looking intensely at us from somewhere out of our range of vision.

Her heart leaped with new strength at the sight of John. They met face to face on the hospital steps, their eyes reading each other's, their love reaching out to offer support.

"Haim's gone?" John asked gently.

"Yes, Daniel and I got here just in time. I was up at your house. I talked with Cynthia," Hannah said breathlessly.

"She's leaving on the steamer down there at the wharf. She came back unexpectedly to collect her things. I'm very sorry I was not here with Haim when you arrived, but I've been with him as much as I could. But, Hannah, how did you get back so quickly? Did you get my telegram? And how did you get up through that fog last night? Come on into my office where we can talk for a minute."

Inside John's office Hannah dropped her heavy bag. As she explained how she came home early, she felt the years fall off her shoulders.

"Your telegram must have arrived after I left Montreal. I began to feel restless at Belle's, more so every hour. As soon as we could, we set out to make our way back. Noah was going to bring us up this morning, the fog being too heavy last night. But I just knew I had to get up here one way or another. And so Daniel and I set out on foot with a lantern. We made it in a bit over six hours. Oh, John, I'm so thankful we managed to make the long trek up to see dear Haim. He was able to speak with us. It has cleared up something important for Daniel."

John took Hannah into a warm embrace and held her closely, sharing his strength with her, adding his stamina and steadfastness to hers.

Hannah smiled. "I'm going back to Daniel now."

"I'm coming with you. I want to see him."

Daniel was sitting on a long wooden bench with Ky Henson, who was upset by Haim's rapid demise. John laid a hand on Daniel's shoulder and the boy rose, standing nearly as tall as the doctor. They talked in the easy, comfortable way of old friends. Then John excused himself to sign Haim's death certificate.

John was about to leave the death room when he noticed that Haim's things, including his yellow clock, still had to be packed, and so he set about the task, wishing to spare Hannah further anguish.

The sight of the brass chain bracelets sent a wave of compassion through him and he stopped for a few moments to think about Haim's life of struggle and illness. But he also remembered that Haim's married years had been graced with Hannah's love.

Just as John was coming out of the room, Hannah was going in for a few last moments alone with Haim.

After a while two orderlies carried Haim's shrouded body in a plain pine box on a stretcher to the waiting steamer. John walked behind Haim's body with Hannah and Daniel. As the little party moved away from the hospital, John saw Cynthia starting down from his house. Hannah looked at the woman John had loved balancing unevenly on her high heels as she walked behind the night watchman who was struggling to keep her voluminous luggage on his hand cart.

John gazed into Hannah's eyes with intensity, then took his leave of her and Daniel to walk down to the steamer with Cynthia.

The Captain of the steamer came forward to offer his sympathy and to escort Hannah and Daniel to a private cabin. Peering out through a porthole, Daniel saw Noah Speke looking for them on the wharf.

"There's Uncle Noah, Ma. He must have just arrived. I'll go tell him about Pa." And Daniel raced away down the corridor, finding release for his grief in the process of running.

Hannah was deep in thought when she heard footsteps coming toward her cabin door. A second later John's frame filled the doorway. He kissed Hannah tenderly, then gently took his leave to have a parting word with Daniel.

Noah stood awkwardly before Hannah and shook his head sadly. "I'm some sorry, Hannah, my maid. But I'll make the coffin, look. Oh, and if ye haven't already done it, I'll speak to the Reverend Coates about taking the funeral, sure. Oh, and, Hannie, what a walk ye must have had to get up here t'rough that fog! Ye're some brave soul, I've always known that." With that, Noah disembarked to take his open fishing boat back to Steadman's Cove.

The ship's engine shuddered and Hannah felt the steamer pulling away from the dock to take up its southward course. She wanted to peer out of the porthole, to have one last look at John, but she sat pensively on the edge of a bunk.

They reached the Cove before word of Haim's death had come south and so there was no one to meet them. One of the sailors came forth to help Daniel carry his father's body in its crude box to the Holt house.

And so the little village of Steadman's Cove was in mourning once again. This time it grieved for their beloved Haim, cut from his moorings prematurely at the age of forty-two.

Chapter Twenty-four

For Hannah the days after Haim's funeral dragged past in a numbingly weary procession. Where, she wondered, were the angel wings which had hovered around her after Morna's death, cheering her on to take up her life once more? Where was the radiant power that she knew had become part of her the morning she fell and rose again on the Point?

As the autumn turned into winter, Hannah felt like a bird that had missed out on migration; the feet that were stuck in September's mud were now frozen fast in December's snow. In fact she did not even feel like writing in her diary. But one day, after she had come back from seeing that Haim's dogs were distributed around the village and that food and blankets were taken down to the tilt, the old urge to write came over her again.

It was then Hannah realized she had not actually seen her diary since Haim's death. She searched everywhere for the book into which she had freely poured her most intimate thoughts, but she could not find it. When her inner turmoil had subsided, when her feelings of mortification at the thought of someone else reading her poems, dreams and confessions had eased up, she concluded that she must have lost the diary on the tough trek to Haim. Possibly when she set down her bag to knock the sharp point off High Rock; or, heaven forbid, could it have dropped out of her bag when she was in John's office?

After Haim's death, Hannah half expected that John would just appear at her door one day. But her expectations were shadowed by rumours. Twyla Henson said Dr. John had taken ill and left the coast for good.

Turning her energy toward painting and papering the house, Hannah completed the project she had started while Haim was still alive. She rearranged Haim's hand-hewn pieces of pine furniture against walls of fresh white and pale yellow. Here and there she laid down the warm reds and blues of Daniel's hooked mats. On the walls she hung his paintings. So vigorously did she spend her restlessness on decorating the home, there was little room left for the anger and guilt that often haunt the bereaved. Hannah lost herself in emptying the house of every useless oddment, all the scraps saved and never used, including old yellow almanacs that had foretold the future of days gone by.

During that long autumn Will helped the men with the fishing, taking Daniel along in his boat. After his father's death, Daniel was determined to help earn his own and his mother's keep. It would have been easy for him to spend all his days working with Emma, who was intrigued with the patterns for creating family trees which he had brought back from Montreal. Emma had so touted the idea that every family should have its own family tree that women in the Cove were stitching the names of their forebears on the best pieces of fabric they could afford. With a growing optimism that they would one day have their own store in the Bight, Emma and Daniel added steadily to their stockpile of crafts.

Hannah was often tempted to go up to the Bight for a day, just to see for herself what was happening with John. But she waited until early December when Will took her and Daniel to the hospital for chest X-rays because of their close contact with Haim's miliary tuberculosis. Fortunately, their X-rays were both clear, to their quiet relief.

On that December morning in the year 1948, while Will took Daniel into the village to return the books he had borrowed from the secondary school principal the previous summer, Hannah knocked on the door of John's office.

"Dr. Weatherton's gone out for the winter," said the secretary. "He won't be back until some time in the spring. There's a new doctor to look after his work. Is there anything I can do for you?"

"Nothing, thank you." And Hannah walked dejectedly down the corridor, feeling as though some personal sun had set forever, for she remembered John's promise to let her know when he was going away. The concern that he might have taken ill, too ill to send her a message, soon eclipsed her feelings of having been slighted.

Hannah was just about to sit down in the waiting room when she heard someone walking behind her. Turning around, she saw the same secretary waving a letter and a parcel wrapped in heavy brown paper.

"Here's a letter Dr. John left for you. Joanna and Dr. Andrew were supposed to have taken it to you back in October, but they completely forgot. You know what people are like when they're in love."

Hannah tore open the envelope and eagerly read the letter in John's handwriting:

3 October 1948

Hannah dear:

I hope this letter reaches you as I plan it to — from the hands of Joanna and Andrew. As it turns out, I'm leaving the coast in a bit of a rush because a substitute doctor has just arrived to do a locum tenens *for me and I must make the most of the time he is here. I'm leaving this afternoon on a steamer.*

I want to settle my divorce as quickly as possible.

212

Also I need to brush up on my professional skills and so I'm going to spend some time at Harvard — studying and also giving some lectures on frontier medicine and the current status of tuberculosis in northern Newfoundland.

I wish I weren't going out at this time when I might be of some comfort to you, dear Hannah. I'm finding it hard to pack — keep forgetting some things, misplacing others. Will you understand when I say I feel as though I'm leaving a part of myself behind? Will you understand when I ask you to be careful about going out to the Point?

One day, when you were out in Montreal, I walked your path to that beautiful height you love. I could appreciate what a superhuman effort you must have made to scale that wall of granate (sic) up to safety again. (But there's little can surprise me now about you — now that I realize that you and Daniel made that trek to Haim's bedside over the most horrendous bog and through a soupy fog. On that fateful morning, when Haim died and Cynthia was just leaving, it didn't make quite the impression it did a few hours later when I had had time to take it all in!)

I can understand why you love to walk to that great windswept height, to look out over the vast ocean. I looked back at the little Cove, then westward toward you and Daniel out in Montreal and I sent you waves of loving good wishes.

Oh, and on the way up to the Point I looked in the windows of your old school and imagined you as a little girl. I strolled through "your" church too and pictured you as a bride. But the crown of my "Hannah pilgrimage" was standing up on the Point where you must have stood so often, refreshing your soul.

Do you understand why I wanted to walk where

you had walked, see what you had seen, feel the rusty wire holding the cemetery gate — as you had done? Isn't this the way of those who love?

I want you to put your mind at ease about Haim for he was blissfully free of both fear and pain during his last days. He spoke so lovingly of you, dear Hannah, and he seemed to know you would come back early. Difficult though it is, we have to let those we love be free, even in death. . . .

Free Advice Department:*Whatever you do, don't try to spend all of your grief in hard work. I can tell you, it doesn't work. Grief takes its own time. Don't be afraid to be angry, to weep — for only when you've let yourself go through what is yours to go through can you begin to laugh and love again. Listen to the radio — to music, not just the news. Oh, and I'm leaving a box of books with my secretary for your winter reading.*

The book wrapped in so many layers of paper is, I believe, your diary. It must have fallen from your bag the morning Haim died. It was under my desk. I recognized the family photos that fell out. I immediately wrapped it up for this package so that you would have the relief of having it back in your own hands, knowing no one had read it — not even I!

Dear Hannah, take care of yourself this winter. You and Daniel won't forget to have your chest X-rays taken, will you? I'll see you in April.

Please know I think of you often. In the meantime, I'm enclosing a forwarding address.

Affectionately,
John

Hannah tucked the letter in her bag. She hurried down to the secretary and asked her for some paper and an envelope.

In the time that remained before the boys returned, she
wrote:

Up at the Bight
9 December 1948

Dear John:
I was so happy to get your letter today when Daniel
and I came up for our chest X-rays. (All clear.)
Your secretary has just given it to me, two months
after you wrote it. I understand the delay. It ends
my worries during the long autumn of wondering
what had happened to you. I had even heard you
were ill. Thanks be to God you're well.
I have a little gift I found for you in Montreal.
I'll take it up to Abigail to await your return.
Thanks for leaving me more books. They will help
me through this forlorn winter.
By the time you return, we'll officially be part of
Canada! Haim would have had tumbled feelings about
all the talk and predictions as to what's to become
of us. But we have our good backbones and we'll
come through.
I'm deeply grateful for what you did to ease
Haim's last days on earth. With blessings for good
travelling as well as my deep affection.
As ever,
Your loving friend,
Hannah

P.S. Do you know why people put an x at the end
of a letter? Seems like in the olden days, when
fewer people could write, a person might sign
his or her name with an x. Over the years the
x came to stand for the seal of sincerity.
x HH

John's loving letter lifted Hannah's spirits during that first
long winter of her widowhood – and she reread it often.
The more time Daniel spent working with Emma on crafts,
the more Hannah wondered how much longer she wanted
to live in the Cove. The almost empty nest made her aware
of her own inner emptiness and she made up her mind that
one day she would move to St. John's to study at Memorial
University College.

That Christmas Daniel and Hannah joined the Spekes
for dinner. Noah had shot a fine hare and Belle had sent a
crate of oranges on the last steamer. They all missed both
Haim and Morna that first Christmas after their deaths
within such a short time of one another.

In the days between Christmas and Old Christmas on
January 6, Will and Daniel took part in the ancient practice
of mummering often observed in the outports. Disguised in
old clothes or bed sheets, they went from door to door
singing the old songs. Often someone had a mouth organ
and the men would dance with the women in a house.

In some coves mummering was used to "get a message
across" to someone. The message might have been directed
to a merchant who had been observed during the year resting his thumb on his scale while weighing out a customer's
purchase. Sometimes they drifted a message toward a
neighbour who had "borrowed" someone's wheelbarrow
on a rather permanent basis. Mummering was an old
custom designed to clear the air of tensions accumulated
during the year in a tightly knit community. Its more

serious purpose was always wrapped in jokes, laughter and good fun.

The day after Christmas Noah and Haim had always made their "weather almanacs." On this particular Christmas Noah decided it was time for Daniel and Will to understand the ancient way of predicting the weather for the year ahead. He taught the boys to observe the direction of the wind for twelve days after Christmas. "The twelve days stand for the next twelve months. I've never failed to know when the coast would be clear of h'ice in the spring or be forming up in the fall."

Will and Daniel had seen enough of the Newfoundland wisdom to pay heed to Noah's own time-tested folklore.

The annual Sports Day came and went without Hannah's paying much attention to it. When she was not listening to the radio for news of union with Canada, she tuned in to classical music from the British Broadcasting Corporation. That was the winter she rediscovered Mahler's often mystifying music; it seemed to match her mood of longing and uncertainty. Music was her way of reaching out to John.

Then came the unsettling day when Daniel announced to his mother that he was going out to the sealing ice with Will and Noah.

A shock wave of agony swept through Hannah. Silently she moved over to the stove and dusted off the lids with the old mother-angel goose wing. She remembered Morna once saying: "Sometimes there's nothing for it but for us women to go ahead and wait!" Lifting a stove lid, Hannah shoved more wood into the flames. Certainly they needed the money since her midwifery paid little or nothing. But beyond the need for income was Daniel's necessity to slay his personal dragon, if not the seals. Hannah understood that to interfere was to risk damaging her son's passage to manhood.

"I want to bring in some money for our keep, Ma. Who

knows? Maybe next year I'll work at summat else to help out," Daniel said earnestly.

Then Will spoke up on behalf of his friend. "It's been arranged that Daniel will pile and keep track of the pelts, recording how many each man killed. Daniel will be an executive at the hunt and I promise you, Mrs. Holt, I'll see that everything's fair and square for Daniel. He'll be there for the count, but not the kill. Won't be like last year."

On February 7 of that year — 1949 — Canada's Prime Minister Louis St. Laurent introduced legislation concerning confederation of Newfoundland. The island hummed with talk and the village of Steadman's Cove counted the days until many of its citizens would go north to Barton's Bight to celebrate the island's officially becoming Canada's tenth province on March 31.

The Holts and the Spekes went up to the Bight on two dog teams with their shakedowns and sleeping bags, for they were planning to stay overnight with friends. The Bight was bustling with visitors from neighbouring hamlets. The community hall filled early on that historic evening, with the young men perched up on the high beams and rafters. Someone led a chant that declared, "Now that we're in, we'll never be able to get out!" The mayor of the Bight gave an impassioned speech about the privilege of being Canada's tenth province, while the senior dignitaries wore silk top hats rented from St. John's.

At the stroke of midnight, that moment when confederation with Canada was official, all hats were tossed up in the air amid hoots, shouts and whistles. The next morning Newfoundlanders awoke to the reality of being part of Canada with mixed feelings. And understandably some were more enthusiastic about it than others. But it was not long until they were urging each other to forget their differences and to try to make union a great success.

The celebration of confederation passed, leaving Hannah

feeling as numb as she did during her long, sad autumn. She wondered if John had received her letter. But after many weeks of contemplating her future, she was once again swept up in looking after the people of the Cove.

With Haim's death, her life had changed. Even her friendship with Emma was different, for her old friend was rushing off to this village and that, stirring up interest in arts and crafts. Both the Ranger and Ben Brack had called on Hannah from time to time, preying on her loneliness and making their lecherous intentions clear. But Hannah politely discouraged them both.

She took even more walks out to the Point, to the great concern of Noah, who felt a neighbourly responsibility for Hannah. One day late in April, when Noah was just coming up from the wharf, he saw Hannah striding out to the Point again and he ran to catch up with her.

"Hannah, my love, d'ye think ye take too many walks to the Point? I'm mortal afeart ye'll take another tumble like yon one ye had before."

"Don't worry yourself about me, Noah. A walk's a good way to clear the heart," Hannah said with a smile.

Concerned for Hannah, Noah walked with her to the Point. Once at the top, however, he could not conceal his own great fear of heights as the wind whipped around them.

On that same afternoon John was on his way back to Newfoundland, flying from Boston to Gander via Montreal with plans to sail north to the Bight from Gander on a coastal steamer. It was while John was checking in at Montreal's Dorval airport that he noticed a tall, distinguished-looking older man with eagle-lean features and bright-blue eyes. In a flash John noticed a striking resemblance to Hannah. As the man turned to leave the counter, John also observed the man's wistful faraway look. Then John drew himself up short. In his intense longing for Hannah, he wondered if he were becoming overly imaginative.

But then, as they boarded the plane, John noticed a small discreet sticker depicting the yellow-and-blue flag of Sweden affixed to one corner of the man's attaché case.

Intrigued now, John slipped into the aisle seat alongside the man. As they jostled their hand luggage under their seats, they made the opening polite gambits that invite further conversation.

"I see from the flag on your case that you're from Sweden," John ventured.

"Yes," the man replied with a precise Swedish accent. "I'm from Stockholm. I've just been out to visit my daughter in Toronto. I'm flying to Gander en route to Sweden via London." Then the man smiled politely, nodded and closed his eyes until lunch was served.

John noticed that the Swede ate little lunch. It was over coffee that the older man asked, "Are you flying to London too?"

"No, sir. I'm on my way back to northern Newfoundland. I'm a doctor at a place called Barton's Bight. By the way, my name is Weatherton."

"And mine is Jensen," the man said, his face alive with interest. "I'm a retired sea captain now, but when I was on the seas I once put into a little cove up there. Quite near Barton's Bight. Can't recall its name."

"The only village called a cove up that way is Steadman's Cove. Would that be it?" John asked tentatively.

"I believe it is. Thought I'd never forget the name of that place. The people were so kind. I actually had a very good week there. That must have been thirty years ago now." And the man gazed off into space.

Closer to thirty-six years, John mused to himself, almost certain now that this distinctive-looking man was Hannah's father. And yet his clinical training cautioned him against putting credence in what might be mere coincidence.

Then the sea captain reached into his pocket for his

wallet. "Here is a photograph of my daughter and my grandchildren," he said proudly.

John took the picture and studied it longer than one would ordinarily look at a stranger's family photo. But the undeniable likeness of the Toronto woman to Hannah left John astounded.

"Fine-looking girl," John said, recovering himself.

"And just as fine as she looks. Very good to her old father. Your being a doctor, you'll understand my illness. You see, I have a cancer of my pancreas. A matter of time. I just had to see my little family in Toronto. I'm a widower. Have only the one child. . . ."

Only one that you know of, John thought, as he offered his sympathetic support to the sea captain making his last voyage — this time by air. Even the way Jensen tilted his head as he spoke was uncannily similar to Hannah's characteristic gesture.

John had loved the one letter he had received from Hannah. He had responded to her from Boston, but having received no reply, John assumed the letter had not reached her yet. Sitting beside the man who John was sure had fathered Hannah intensified his longing to hold her in his arms, to taste the freedom that would surely now be theirs.

At Gander airport the two men took a quietly emotional leave of each other, lingering over their handshake. Then they went their separate ways, both looking back at the same moment to wave a final farewell.

Aboard the coastal steamer bound for Barton's Bight, John thought about the brave, lonely man he had just met. He decided not to mention the incident to Hannah since the news could only be upsetting to her. But in his heart, he knew. As he gazed out through the gathering mists of dusk, John appreciated again the truth that nothing in this life happens by chance alone.

Chapter Twenty-five

Meanwhile, back in Steadman's Cove Hannah's spirits began to lift with the spring sunshine. She took a new interest in what she might do with her life. The benefits of confederation with Canada were becoming apparent in the northern villages. Optimism rose among both the old and the young. For one thing, the elderly could now count on receiving thirty dollars a month for their pension. The families with large numbers of children did well on the Family Allowance — much better than on the uncertain income from fishing.

Drifting up from the South were distorted tales of the stubborn anti-confederates, still half singing, half weeping about the wolfish jaws of the St. Lawrence having swallowed up their island. Life, they said, would never be as good again. For them, this was undoubtedly true. But for many of the outport fisherfolk, life would never be as bad again.

Certainly union with the mainland was helping Daniel and Emma, who now had cash with which to buy craft supplies and even pay some of their workers a little each month. Daniel's girl friend, Mary Williams, helped them too by finding a market for their creations in St. John's. That was the spring of 1949, and Will Speke sent off his application to medical school at McGill University.

As her appetite for living improved, Hannah regained some of her weight. One day she opened the burgundy luggage Belle had bought when they were in Montreal. To her amazement, it was filled with clothes and cosmetics. Hannah could not imagine where Belle ever thought she would wear the exquisite lingerie, blouses, pretty dresses, pleated skirts, but she tried them all on, rubbed the rich creams on her face and dabbed perfumes on her wrists.

While folding the clothes in her bureau, Hannah came across the colourful kite given to Daniel by the remorseful boy in Montreal, and she sent it drifting through the bedroom, imagining it soaring into the sky above the Point.

A few days later Hannah awakened to a clear, sunny day and she knew it was the perfect time to fly the kite. She hurried down the stairs from her bedroom in the loft and knocked on Daniel's door.

"Daniel, my boy, would you like to see how your kite looks sailing out over the Point?"

Hannah led the way to a protected plateau where Daniel could catch his first glimpse of the seascape she loved.

"Ah, 'tis marvellous up here, Ma. Another world altogether. I can see why you like to come out, but I can also see why Pa worried ye might fall." Daniel scanned the rocky cliff. "That place up there must be where ye fell from a year ago."

"That's the spot, my son. But let's come back in a bit to send the kite up. We'll have our own private celebration about confederation with Canada. So here's to us all, Danny, my boy."

It was a perfect place to fly the kite. The wind was strong and constant. Secure in his footing, Daniel gazed in wonder at the colourful kite soaring against a clear blue sky. "Can fair feel the tug of the wind right up my arm," he said.

Hannah savoured a triumphant moment of sharing with Daniel what she herself loved. Above all, she wanted him to find the courage of the sea within himself, a power to be with him forever.

"Look, Ma!" Daniel called out as he began to wind in the kite. "There's Dr. John coming around that inlet!"

Hannah looked down to see John leaning out of the wheelhouse of his small boat as he brought it steadily in toward the lighthouse-keeper's wharf.

"Let's go, Ma. I can't wait to see him," Daniel said, expressing Hannah's own feelings.

Together they made their way down the rocky slope, Hannah in the lead. Daniel put his hand on Hannah's shoulder and they made a game of the descent down the path. John had already tied his boat and was running toward them. Hannah stepped aside, letting Daniel be the first to greet John.

"Welcome home, Dr. John! You're in Canada now, y'know."

John took Daniel in his arms, then held him by the shoulders, studying the young man's face. "Oh, Daniel, it's good to see you again! And what a height you've grown to."

Daniel took in a deep breath as he did when he was at a loss for words to match his feelings. He smiled at John, then turned to his mother and stepped back.

Hannah stretched out her hands to John, the palms turned upward in warm welcome. Words seemed superfluous. They kissed each other tenderly then rested their heads on each other's shoulders in a lingering embrace, uninhibited by Daniel's presence.

"I've missed you, Hannah," John said, feasting on the sight of her fine porcelain features. "I'm only just back on the coast. Had to go south on a call this morning and was on my way to the Cove when I saw the two of you up there with the kite. What a beautiful reunion!"

Then John put his arms around Hannah and Daniel, guiding them down toward his boat. "I've an idea," he said enthusiastically. "Let's have lunch aboard my boat. Now that I have an assistant at the hospital, I don't have to rush back. If you two are free, we can sail up the shore and drop anchor some place. What do you say to that?"

Delighted at the invitation, Hannah and Daniel climbed aboard. They dropped anchor at a small grassy inlet south of the Cove. And while John grated the cheese and Hannah whipped up the eggs for an omelette, Daniel took off on his own to explore the boat. In the cramped quarters of the galley, it was natural enough for John and Hannah to slip into each other's arms again until the acrid smell of burning omelette brought them back to the task at hand.

John thanked Hannah for her letter and the book of Santayana's writings. "I missed you so much this winter."

"It was a long, lonely autumn, John. Worst of all were the rumours. That you'd left the coast for good. That you'd had a heart attack. That you'd gone out to find a new wife. But then I got your letter."

They took their lunch to the deck where they looked out on a rocky shoreline, brightened here and there by a struggling patch of green. To Hannah's embarrassment, Daniel did most of the talking. But John encouraged the boy and told him to be sure to come up to the Bight for another summer. After lunch, they sailed on up toward Steadman's Cove. As they drew alongside the wharf, they saw numerous rain-washed photographs of Joseph Small-wood, Newfoundland's new Premier, with the still-legible words: *He's our saviour, Joey is!*

Hannah invited John up to the house for coffee. On their way they met Will Speke, who thanked John for his letter of reference and told him he had sent in his application to McGill medical school. While the two boys walked down into the village, John and Hannah went in to her home.

John took a long, lingering look around the rooms. "Hannah, whatever have you done to the place? It doesn't look the same at all!"

"I painted and papered away my loneliness," Hannah

said, putting on the kettle. "At first I thought of moving out to Montreal as soon as Daniel was settled somewhere. Then I knew I didn't really like the city very much and I began to think about St. John's where I could work part-time and study at Memorial University. That's where my plans are now. But I wanted to fix up the house as a place to come back to."

John rested his hands on Hannah's shoulders while he looked steadily into her bright blue eyes.

"My darling, you can't be seriously thinking of leaving the North. Why, you're the main reason I'm back here. I was offered a position in Boston, but I had to come back to you. My divorce is final. Cynthia's getting married again this fall. To her southern gentleman," John said with a touch of tartness.

Hannah turned the two rocking chairs around so they would be closer to each other, but John was not ready to sit down. He swept Hannah into his arms and kissed her passionately on the lips.

"Hannah, I've loved you from the first time I laid eyes on you. I want to marry you, my darling. We're meant for each other."

As they stood together, Hannah looked into John's eyes and gently said, "I want to spend the rest of my days with you."

They parted long enough for John to take a parcel from his bag. Almost shyly he said, "I found this for you in Boston. I hope you like it."

Hannah drew out a beautiful reversible coat — blue and white tweed on one side, dark blue on the other — with a pretty hat to match. She modelled it, strolling around the kitchen, feeling both shy and pleasantly worldly. Then she thanked him warmly with a hug and a kiss.

"It's amazing how easy it is to shop for someone we love," John said philosophically, echoing Hannah's experience when she found just the right gift for him in Montreal.

Hannah was about to take off her new coat when Daniel and Will rushed into the kitchen.

"Dr. John," they said almost in unison, "there's been an accident down at the wharf! Gar Smith's got his arm crushed between a boat and the wharf!"

John went down to examine the man and was back in minutes. "Looks as though Smith's got a fracture. I'm going to take him up to the hospital. Why don't you come along, Hannah? I'll get my housekeeper Abigail to pack us a picnic supper. After I've looked after Gar, we'll sail on up to l'Anse aux Meadows. Then I'll bring you back here later this evening. What do you say to that?"

"I'd love that," Hannah said.

That afternoon she wore her new coat and hat, to John's delight. On the way down to his boat, they met Will and Daniel. The boys whistled at Hannah's new outfit and Will suggested, "Daniel can come to our place for supper, and maybe even stay overnight."

Late that April afternoon John and Hannah sailed north until they reached l'Anse aux Meadows, the theoretical site of an ancient Viking settlement. They walked around the mounds and borders where primitive dwellings may have stood, while John explained various theories about the early Viking explorations.

"Of course, some of the local people think it's just a lot of talk about this ever having been a Viking settlement. But I once stayed in the home of a fisherman nearby and he was convinced that the early Vikings landed here. He predicted that one day someone from away would come and excavate the whole thing."

Hannah realized that John had brought her here because her father was Scandinavian. It gave her a feeling of pride to think that her ancestors may have discovered northern Newfoundland.

No words were needed in that moment as they stood together, arm in arm, looking toward an orange sun dropping down in the west and casting long shadows over the mounds. When Hannah began to shiver, they hurried back to the warmth of John's boat and opened their picnic supper. They lighted candles and enjoyed their sandwiches with a bottle of white wine. They talked about their months apart, wanting to know everything about each other and needing to tell everything about themselves.

"Sometimes I was so lonely," Hannah said, "that I used to put the kettle on just to hear it hum."

Slowly and gently Hannah felt her old wedding band coming off and a new ring going on in its place. She opened her eyes to see a diamond reigning supremely above a band of gold.

"John, it's so beautiful," she said as she turned it back and forth on the tender skin so long protected by Haim's broad wedding band.

"I bought it in good faith in Boston, trusting you had not run off with the Ranger, or what's that bachelor's name? Ben Brack!" John teased Hannah, who looked from the diamond sparkling in the light of the candle to John's vulnerable gaze.

"And does this mean we might get married one day?" Hannah asked with the playful innocence of a child.

"Why should we wait? What's to keep us from getting married next month?"

They studied a calendar in John's log book and chose the third Saturday of May.

"I have one more surprise," John said, cradling Hannah in his arms. "Do you remember the sick sea captain we brought in off his ship one night a year ago? Well, just before I left last fall, he sent me a gift. It's a passage for two to France, where we can stay in his cottage on the Riviera!"

They went to take a last look over the Viking ruins. While Hannah felt her feet firmly planted on the soil her Scandinavian forebears might have trod, John thought of the Swedish sea captain he believed was Hannah's father.

Between the fading light of the sun and the early rays of the moon glinting on the North Atlantic waters, they sailed south to Steadman's Cove.

Closer to the Cove Hannah asked, "Would you like to stay over at the house tonight?"

"That sounds like a good idea. It is a bit late to sail back up to the Bight."

Hannah turned to look back at the setting sun then forward toward the moon. "I don't believe you and I will ever play the old marital game of one being the sun, the other the moon," she said.

"With occasional total eclipses?" John asked, understanding what Hannah was thinking. "No, we'll just be each other's light."

"And each other's warmth," Hannah added with a toss of her head while they came alongside the wharf at Steadman's Cove.

As they walked toward the village in the gathering dusk, Hannah noticed that her house was brightly lighted.

"Daniel must be home," she said.

Hannah knocked at the door, feigning formality as she turned and smiled at John. Then they walked into the kitchen together. Seated at the table were Daniel and Will playing checkers. Newly made calendars for the months of May through September lay nearby.

John picked up the calendar for the month of May and boldly circled the third Saturday in red. Then he handed it to Daniel and Will, who looked up in confusion.

"That's the day your mother and I are going to be married," John said, putting an arm around Hannah.

Daniel and Will rose, upsetting their checkers and chairs

in their excitement. Their faces shone with joy at the happy news.

"So this is my new pa! 'Tis the proper t'ing, Ma!" Daniel said as he shook John's hand. Holding his mother's hand to the light to look at the ring, he said, "Whew! Just look at that!"

To Will the love between John and Hannah had a special significance for they had helped him to know he could do whatever he wished with his life and now he embraced them both warmly.

Wrapping a towel around a hot stone from the stove, Hannah slipped it into the guest-room bed. Then she lighted a lamp for John and went back to say good night to Will, who was just leaving for home.

That night sleep was far away for Hannah. Eventually she dozed off, but then she was suddenly awake again, aware of John tossing on a noisy bedspring. Noticing that his lamp was burning, she climbed down to see if he was all right.

"I'm just restless tonight," John said, looking at Hannah's breasts, soft and full under a nightgown of pale-blue satin.

John drew Hannah down to cradle a full, warm breast in his hand. He shifted to draw himself up, taking her in his arms. Suddenly his feet sent the hot stone flying out of the bed to shatter the quiet of the night.

At that moment Daniel called out in his sleep. Hannah kissed John good night, leaving his room just as Daniel appeared sleepily from his bedroom.

"I've had such a dream, Ma! I dreamt a whole shipload of h'ice came through the roof of our house, look. 'Twas so real."

John quietly extinguished his lamp and drew up the covers while he listened to Hannah saying, "There's no hole in the roof and no ice around here, sure, Daniel. Now you'd better go back to your bed."

"But it seems like a night for being awake. Such an exciting time. Hearing about you and Dr. John. . ."

Hannah tucked Daniel back into bed and climbed once again to the loft, smiling to herself as she remembered one September morning in Montreal. She had awakened early and looking down on the garden noticed that the magnolia tree which had bloomed in the spring now offered another cluster of autumn blossoms at the very top of the tree.

Chapter Twenty-six

The wedding day dawned fresh and clear. Hannah stretched and awakened from a dream in which it was her task to pick her way up a seemingly endless stem whose thorns served as ladder-rungs. By the time she reached the top she had learned how to climb the ladder thorns without either breaking them under her weight or pricking her fingers. After the painstaking climb to the top, Hannah dreamed she was floating around a beautiful gold-pink rose glowing from within itself. She saw the pink petals turn a violet shade, then take wing, always being replaced by others.

So real was the struggle up the stem that Hannah looked at her hands for any trace of scratches. Seeing only the beautiful ring from John, she felt like a princess. She raised the window blind to a bright-blue sky and sunlight sparkling on the harbour sea.

Already the Cove bustled with an excitement surpassing even the day that celebrated confederation with Canada. Hannah smiled as she watched Twyla Henson hang a wreath of pink and blue flowers on the church door.

That spring, in the weeks before their wedding day, Hannah and John had seen each other as often as their work permitted. But their trysts were consistently interrupted by one crisis or another and the rarity of their encounters only heightened their passion as they awaited the third Saturday of May.

Hannah went downstairs to make herself a cup of tea. Just as she turned to put the kettle on, she noticed an envelope peeking under the door. Delighted at recognizing John's handwriting, she took the letter and the tea back up to bed to savour its contents.

Some days earlier John had left the letter with Will, to be delivered to Hannah's door during the pre-nuptial night. She tore open the envelope and read:

My darling Hannah:

In only a few hours from the moment your eyes read this letter you and I shall be one with each other, ending the loneliness we have both known. I write this letter to be an extra guardian angel with you during your last hours in the Cove.

As I kiss the fingertips that hold these pages, I write to say I love you utterly — with a fervour I could never have imagined before I came to know and began to understand you.

You may have had a wakeful night, my darling, and this morning may find you filled with a mixture of sad and happy feelings as you leave behind what has been dear and familiar to you. But look out toward the Point (having walked out there, I share it with you) and feel again its rocky timelessness — as enduring as my love for you.

My beloved Hannah, you have brought an ecstacy to my life I could never have imagined possible. I count the hours until we are together, dear heart. In writing these few words, I join the long line of those who have struggled to find the perfect sentence to carry their love to a beloved. But this afternoon, when we are to be together forever more, our love will find its own words, its own wings.

In these last hours until we meet, I shall go to the hospital as little as possible, for increasingly my mind

can hold only thoughts of you. Now I understand
clearly how a man could be martyred for love!
Yours, truly yours,
John

Tears filled her eyes as she reread the letter and then kissed it back in its envelope, marvelling at John's awareness of the feelings of finality existing within a woman on her wedding day. She gazed out toward the Point where Haim and Morna and little Amity were laid to rest. Was he also aware that the wedding day brings a death of the woman-maiden, whatever her age? Did he know what the Greeks understood, that there is a sacrificial aspect to marriage, with a potential for the loss of liberty, uniqueness, as well as a loss of virginity of spirit — to be veiled by the merry sounds of the wedding supper, eventually to be balanced by the law of love whereby love begets love.

As Hannah sipped her tea and thought of John, she listened in her imagination to the lively strains of Greig's "Wedding Day." The precise and perky passages hummed through her mind until she pictured the Nordic women with garlands of red and blue flowers crowning their heads and matching posies embroidered on their blouses. She saw the flying feet of the dancers shod in laced boots and she heard the great pole being brought down on the dance floor again and again, keeping the dancers' bodies moving to the beat of the primal Scandinavian rhythms. It was music that Hannah had often enjoyed on the BBC radio programs, music that stirred her soul.

Naturally enough, on her wedding morning her thoughts turned to her father. Was he still alive? she wondered. What would it be like to walk down the aisle on his arm?

Hannah let her thoughts pour through her, denying none of them until she could once again think only of John. Then she jumped out of bed, drew on her dressing gown and hurried down the ladder-stairs to the kitchen.

It was time Daniel was up and she turned on the radio to some lively music. No need to worry about saving the radio battery for the evening news since no one would be there to hear it. She heated up extra water on the stove for the rudimentary shower which Will and Daniel had built that winter.

She was pressing Daniel's new Montreal suit when Emma rushed in the door, all smiles, with one hand wreathed in a coronet of tiny paper rosebuds to match the blue of Hannah's wedding dress.

That afternoon John sailed to the Cove from Barton's Bight with the minister, Wilbur Coates. John stood up at the altar, handsome in a navy-blue pinstripe suit, white shirt and his Harvard tie. It was the first time Hannah had seen him in a suit, and at the sight of him waiting for her at the end of the aisle, she felt a shiver pass through her body.

Emma pumped out the Wedding March on the wheezy organ as Hannah started up the aisle on Daniel's arm. When she reached John's side, she smiled and gazed steadfastly into his eyes.

Daniel solemnly gave away his mother in marriage to John, who slowly slipped another ring on Hannah's finger. They kissed affectionately, John cradling Hannah's head in his hand. Slowly they turned and walked arm in arm down the aisle, smiling at friends who filled the little church.

Outside, Noah and some of the men soon raised their rusty old muzzle-loaders, sending off salvos of shots into the sky to salute the bride and groom. Emma and the other women squealed with joy as they showered Hannah and John with paper rose petals, while a fiddler led the wedding party into the community hall for the biggest dinner and dance the people of Steadman's Cove had ever seen.

Hannah and John stood just inside the hall, a few feet away from the caribou head mounted over the door, and one after the other the friends from the Cove shook their hands and wished them "God's well." Then John led

Hannah out to the floor to begin the dancing with an old-fashioned waltz, their bodies sliding in a rhythmic union until impulsively he swept her up in his arms and carried her from the dance floor amid loud stampings and whistles and calls of "Hannah and John!" "John and Hannah!"

It was close to midnight when the bride and groom said good-bye to their friends and started to leave the hall. But the couple did not get away without the fiddlers and accordionists escorting them to John's boat. They were about to escape when out of the shadows sprang Daniel and Will, shouting, "Surprise, surprise!" Daniel handed his mother a package wrapped in pink paper. "'Tis something for both of you to have in your home."

Will and Daniel came aboard and watched while John unwrapped the gift of a hooked mat, whose design John and Hannah remembered with joy.

"Would you look at that!" John said, holding the mat out for Hannah to see. "Didn't I draw that scene of a tilt in the woods over a year ago?" John put his arm around Hannah's waist and they gazed at the vivid reminder of a memorable night.

While Hannah took tender leave of Daniel and Will, John started up the engine. Then he made his farewells, promising Daniel he would take good care of his mother forever more. Will assured Hannah that his home was now Daniel's also.

As John eased the boat away from the wharf, he shared another surprise with Hannah and the friends in the Cove. He wound up an old gramophone and put on a recording of a medley of Newfoundland folk music. Out over the harbour through the night air drifted the sounds of "Star of Logy Bay," "The Killigrew Soiree," "Squidjiggin' Ground," "I 'se the B'y" and "Feller from Fortune."

Hannah and John saw the tears in each other's eyes as they listened to the calls and cheers from the people who had run down to the edges of the harbour to sing lustily along with the record — now playing the "Ode to Newfoundland."

Then John took his boat out to anchor around a curve just beyond the lighthouse-keeper's home. When he felt Hannah shivering in the spring night air, they went inside, taking with them the old gramophone now playing Beethoven's Moonlight Sonata.

John left the cabin long enough to fetch a bottle of champagne. When he returned, Hannah stood before him in a pale-blue chiffon nightgown. Reaching blindly out to set the bottle of champagne on the counter, he almost dropped it on the floor. But in the end the bottle stayed where he put it, for a moment later he was drawing Hannah down onto the soft, down-filled mattress, gathering her to his gentle warmth.

Wherever he touched her the quiver of brush fire spread throughout her body. One tidal wave after another rose and fell. Then she lay back in John's arms and half dreamed of pale-blue butterflies slowly taking off one after another from somewhere near her heart. As she reached out and touched John's lean, naked body, her hand resting on the thick dark stretch of hair across his tanned chest, she felt a sweet, new shyness.

"'Tis surely a very intimate thing to do," she whispered, and they laughed together as good lovers can laugh with each other. John took her hand and kissed it, folding it in his against his heart. He was not a lover to turn and drift off to sleep, leaving Hannah to ponder her heart by a flickering candle. And so they talked of their wedding day and their dreams of days ahead until the gramophone wound down with the sound of a noisy yawn and John blew out the candle.

It was close to dawn when Hannah awakened to the sweet sound of little waves licking the gunwale. She lay beside John in that dreamy state when ideas, hints, hunches drift up and offer themselves with the gentleness of a brush with an angel's wing. In this state of creative clarity, Hannah accepted a gratuitous gift that she recognized as being uniquely hers.

It was, for Hannah, a golden moment of the deepest happiness for now she knew exactly what her next life task was to be. She also knew that if she failed to follow the grail she had glimpsed, it would be a loss to her and many others. As though responding to the new currents in the air, John stirred in his sleep and drew Hannah's hand to his cheek.

Chapter Twenty-seven

The next morning Hannah and John stood at the wheel as they sailed southward under brilliant blue sunshine. Sliding one arm through his, she whispered, "I think, my darling, that you have a lover's sweet tooth. . . . Is this what it's going to be like being married to you?"

"I promise you, Mrs. W., it'll grow more so by the hour. You'll be ready to mutiny by the time we're halfway to the next village. But listen to who's talking!"

They sailed down to a village where John had arranged to leave the boat for maintenance while they were in Europe and then they boarded a steamer bound for Gander. From there they flew to Montreal to visit Belle and Delbert.

John and Delbert spent a lot of time talking about sailing and they shared a mutual pleasure in the gymnasium, leaving Hannah and Belle free to talk.

The two sisters sat in a living room looking out on the garden where, only nine months earlier, Daniel had sat sketching. Hannah felt like a different person from her autumn self.

"You look so wonderful, Hannie," Belle said. "You and John make a marvellous couple. He's just as delightful as I remember him. Now what are you going to do with yourself? Maybe become a lady of leisure?"

"As a matter of fact, I'm thinking of taking up a new

career," Hannah said, adding with a little laugh, "All I need is a wealthy patron. You see, I'd like to start a library at the Bight. A library with a special room for older people — for those who'd just like a chat, a cup of tea. You know how lonely the elderly can be — even in our wonderful island. Of course I realize some of them can't read, but there'll be helpers who'll teach them or just read to them."

"Oh, Hannie, what an idea that one is," Belle said enthusiastically, taking Hannah's hands in hers. "Ma would have been so proud of you." Then in a moment of sudden, swift recollection, Belle leaned forward and said with a wistful smile, "Remember what Ma used to say: 'Ye have to be the lead dog if ye want to get a change of scenery'!"

"Oh, now I do remember hearing her say that one time," Hannah said, and the two sisters looked deeply into each other's eyes, lovingly remembering their mother. Then Hannah added, "It's a dream that'll need financing. We need a building. Books. Furniture. It'll cost quite a bit."

Belle nodded. "I know what we're going to do. You and John will have a visit with Delbert's mother. It's just the kind of challenge she'd love, particularly if you call it the Simpson Library."

A luncheon was arranged for the next day with Delbert introducing the matter of the library to his mother. Initially she was more interested in seeking John's opinion on her health. And John listened sympathetically. Before the luncheon was over, however, thanks to Mrs. Simpson's generosity and admiring interest, Hannah's dream was on its way to becoming a reality.

That evening John and Hannah embarked on their European holiday, their state room bidding them welcome with flowers, fruits and champagne — compliments of the Simpsons.

The days at sea flowed softly one into another as they played deck games, read to each other and made plans without end. They got all dressed up for the ship's formal dance and one evening they dined at the Captain's table. Some days they hardly had time to leave their state room.

At Marseilles John rented a car and Hannah marvelled at the ease with which he took the Renault through the rush-hour traffic and out onto the road leading to Captain Jacques Gagnon's seaside cottage near Juan-les-Pins. Well away from Marseilles, they drove on until they came upon an inn which held them spellbound.

The inn was like a small castle set back on a garden bordered with chestnut trees about to burst into blossom. Its grey turrets and towers rose elegantly up into the gathering dusk. Hannah had often imagined just such a building, but to see one before her eyes caught her breath. "Oh, it's magnificent!" she said. "Let's have a tower room!"

"We'll find a tower room where I can 'Hold you forever and a day'!" John laughed as he pocketed the car keys and impulsively took Hannah in his arms. She knew again what it meant to live out to the edges of her being and beyond as she felt his love flow around her like a warm, wild wind.

She brushed back the hair at his temple. "How is it you always know just what I want? Or is it that I always want just what you give?"

"I've often wondered how you know what I'm feeling. Everything you do stirs me. I often feel I'm travelling to islands, mountains, lakesides where I've never been before."

In the hotel they found the room of their dreams. A magnificent desk curved into the window of a full, round tower. A lamp with an amber globe sent a warm light through the room. They dressed for dinner, leaving the unpacking to two waiting chambermaids.

As Hannah and John sank into the coral plush of tufted chairs in the dining room, their eyes took in the exposed stone of one wall and the curvaceous legs of the waitresses in short black uniforms with lacy white aprons and caps.

The maitre d' hummed to the soft romantic music as he stepped from table to table, spreading his chubby hands over each couple as though invoking a blessing.

"Bonsoir!" he said enthusiastically, brandishing wine lists, menus and matches with the flourish of an orchestra conductor. Then inclining intimately toward Hannah and John, he said, "Ah, *le bon Dieu* gave the world lovers to light up the dark corners of our lives!" Then he hesitated for a moment, groping for a phrase. "In French we say you look as though you have *pris la clef des champs* — as though you are lovers who have run away with the key to the fields of frolic."

"We're just newly married," John explained with a proud, gentle smile. "We're on our honeymoon."

"Ah, *la lune de miel. Mes félicitations!*" And with a wave of his hand he brought a waiter instantly as though by magic.

"Ah, madame, she is so beautiful," the maitre d' said, flirting with Hannah through John. Within seconds he was back with a complimentary bottle of champagne.

"It's pure magic," Hannah said as they toasted each other to the music of the gentle saxophones and violins.

The next morning they awakened to a tapping at the door, then watched as a maid set up a lavish breakfast tray graced with a bouquet of sweetheart roses.

"*Bon appétit!*" she called cheerily as she glided out of the room.

Feeling a long way from Steadman's Cove, Hannah buried her face in John's shoulder and welcomed his arms around her. Reality had caught up with her fantasies.

They left the inn to drive along the coast of the Ligurian Sea whose waters were sunswept to a brilliant green. Along the road to Juan-les-Pins they stopped from time to time, once to buy themselves bathing suits.

For Hannah, feeling the sun and water on her body was a sensual and invigorating experience. She had learned to swim a little up at an inland pond beyond the Cove, but the water was always cold and the summers were short. Now when John was not playing the role of attentive life-guard, he taught Hannah the sidestroke and how to tread water. Then they dried each other and picnicked on a high peak overlooking the sea.

As they lay beside a bed of wild scarlet poppies, gazing up at the windswept sky, John said, "I've seen this part of France before, but now that I'm here with you, it's as though I'm seeing it for the first time. In fact, since I've come to know you, my love, everything seems to be new. I feel as though I'm twenty again."

Sharing the same carefree mood, Hannah propped herself up on an elbow and, rolling up some dried grass, made a moustache which she playfully tucked under his nose. "Now monsieur is *un gendarme*!"

"Then I'll take you into my custody at once!" But John's sudden hearty sneeze sent the moustache flying into the air. Laughing like children, they eventually gathered them-selves up and set off for Juan-les-Pins.

Captain Gagnon's cottage was small but immaculate and stocked with wines, cheeses and fruit. Leaning against an enormous bottle of preserved cherries stood a note from the Captain, wishing them a happy holiday and promising that he would visit them one day. Soon after their arrival, however, he sent a message that he had been called away to sea again.

Their days and nights tumbled happily one into another. Hannah learned to ride a bicycle, giving them many a laugh as she wobbled through the town. They talked for hours as they lolled on the beach or strolled along the water's edge, sharing their lives and their dreams. They wrote their names in the sand; they fed each other melon in the moonlight. Often they spoke of Hannah's plans for the library. Then came the day when they replenished the Captain's stores and reluctantly turned the key on their golden days of sand and sea.

On the way to Paris they stopped at a goose farm where they watched the "goose wife" force-feeding the fowl to fatten their livers, a process Hannah found disgusting. But she kept her thoughts to herself as John bought some *pâté de foie gras* and a few truffles.

"That's something I've always wanted to see — a goose farm and a truffle operation," John said as they sped north again. "We'll savour these one night in front of the fireplace."

They spent two days in Paris seeing the usual attractions, including a night club with a strip show which, to John's surprise and delight, Hannah enthusiastically reproduced later in their Left Bank hotel room, right down to her last garter!

Chapter Twenty-eight

By the time they had flown back to Gander, John and Hannah were ready to don their sea-going clothes and head north once more. The morning they approached Steadman's Cove on the steamer, the weather was cold and overcast but not foggy, so they were surprised to hear the foghorn booming out at the Point.

"Now what could that mean?" John wondered aloud.

"Oh, they're probably just testing it," Hannah suggested.

But when they reached the Cove they saw people hurrying toward the community hall. Then Hannah slipped an arm through John's and drew him to her as she showed him a sign nailed to a post: *Welcome Home, Hannah and John!*

Daniel and Will swept their luggage out of their hands while Noah and two other fiddlers led a welcoming party up to the community hall. With her arm around Daniel, Hannah thought of an earlier return when, on reaching the wharf there was no smoke rising from their chimney.

Emma hurried to catch up with Hannah and the two locked arms like the school girls they once were. "My, but ye're both looking healthy! Such a heavenly colour of a tan ye've got on your face, my love!"

Once again the villagers had gathered to celebrate Hannah and John with a hearty lunch. When the last teacup was drained, Daniel and Will escorted the newlyweds up to

Hannah's old home. That night Daniel decided he should sleep at the Spekes, as he had done since his mother's marriage. He and Emma were leaving the next day to distribute craft material down the coast.

Hannah and John slept in the guest room, with a hot, towel-wrapped stone at their feet. Holding Hannah tenderly in his arms, John said, "The people of the Cove adore you, my love, and they're surely going to miss you." Hannah took a long, deep breath. For her it was a night for memories to stalk her sleep.

The next morning Hannah arose before John and she slipped quietly out of the bedroom. She looked around the old living room and her eyes came to rest on Haim's clock. Holding it in the palm of her hand, she gently wound it, thinking that it would be a sound to ease the silence of his old home should Daniel come back in a day or so after she and John were gone. But as she wound the yellow clock, she knew she was taking a moment to honour her own and Daniel's memories of Haim.

Later that morning Hannah slowly closed the door of her old home behind her and walked over to join John, who was talking to Will.

"Daniel will be up with you in the Bight just as soon as Ma and he finish with the craft show over on the Straits side," Will said. "Probably in a week or so he and I'll come up to the Bight. And you know, Hannah, that any time Daniel's in the Cove, he has a home with us." Then Will put his arms around Hannah and kissed her on the cheek.

Over Will's shoulder Hannah caught a glimpse of Daniel observing the farewells from behind Emma's lace curtains. She wanted to go to him, to say good-bye in privacy, but something held her where she stood. The curtain fluttered and a few moments later Daniel walked toward his mother, his head up, a smile on his face. He stood between Hannah and John, his arms around their waists. He kissed his mother. Then he kissed John.

"I love you, Ma," Daniel said as he looked into his mother's eyes. He turned to John. "And I love my new pa too!"

It was exactly the benediction Hannah needed to help her leave the Cove with dignity and courage as she said good-bye to Daniel and Will, Emma and Noah, all waving them on their way from the wharf.

At her new home in the Bight, John reached for the door knob, then smiled at Hannah. "Close your eyes, my darling." And they walked hand in hand over the threshold of their new life. Hannah opened her eyes to see John's home decorated in pastels and the colonial wallpaper he had brought back from Boston.

"John, you've changed everything."

"The marital ghosts have been exorcised," he said. Then framing Hannah's face with his hands, taking in every detail of her features, he gazed into her eyes. "Welcome home, my darling Hannah. . . ."

They stood holding each other until Abigail peeked around a door, bearing aloft a partridgeberry pie she had made for the homecoming.

A few nights later John and Hannah were awakened at two in the morning by the racket of spoons banging on pot bottoms, pot lids clanging together and a general hulla-baloo outside their bedroom window.

"What's all that racket?" John asked as they jumped out of bed.

Peering through the window they saw a long stream of townspeople marching toward their door. Hannah burst out laughing at the ancient custom being enacted outside their home.

"We're being shivareed! It's a funny way of telling a couple the community bids them welcome. In return, we're supposed to bring them all in and feed them — still wearing our nightclothes!"

"How do we ever feed them all?" John exclaimed.

Downstairs Abigail, who had known of the scheme in advance, was already spreading a feast. When Hannah and John appeared, the kitchen was filled with bawdy laughter as one by one the revellers wished the couple long, happy years together.

"Now we're truly married," Hannah said as they snuggled back into bed.

During the happy months that followed, Hannah chose the site for the library and defined its role for the community. She designed a fireplace with an ample hearth and window seats curving into bow windows looking out on the harbour.

When the days were warm, Hannah took a chair outside and, sitting with her books and blueprints, she watched for the first glimpse of John striding toward her between the rows of evergreens. No longer did he walk toward a lamp waiting in the window and a dinner heating in the oven. At the first sight of John she hurried to meet him with a rush of love. They would embrace and walk into the house, their arms around each other, their faces turned to read the news of the day in each other's eyes.

Little Ingrid was born the following spring. The christening was to take place as soon as the ice was away for another season. And one Sunday the Reverend Coates, John, Hannah and the baby sailed down to Steadman's Cove to the old Anglican Church where they had been married the year before.

Emma had readied Hannah's old home and brought the cradle down from the loft. She and Daniel lined it with warm covers woven by their own hands. Mary Williams, Daniel's girl friend, home from teachers' college, was Ingrid's godmother. Will Speke, home from his first year as a pre-medical student at McGill, was the godfather.

Daniel could hardly take his eyes off his little half-sister. He shook his head in wonder. "Sure. . .she's some sweet!"

Among the many friends who came to the christening

were Tom and Angie Prynn. The Hensons sat close to the back of the church where Twyla took notes for the local weekly paper, of which she was the editor. Ky's bout with TB had stripped him of his old bombastic self and left him gentle, loving and somewhat inscrutable.

Partway through a lunch of fresh salmon, Noah left the table to present his hand-made gift to Ingrid: a rocking cradle in the shape of a fisherman's dory painted white except for the blue letters of its name: *The Ingrid*.

"See, with the seats out, 'tis a cradle. With the seats in, 'tis a dory. And when she can sit up, she can rock away as though she were out at sea."

Delighted with Noah's gift, Hannah and John tucked Ingrid into her new cradle that night. The next morning Hannah was still asleep when Emma bustled over to make breakfast for them all, setting up a special tray to take upstairs to Hannah while John bathed the baby. The two women laughed and recalled the days when Emma used to say she was "half drave crazy with kids!"

Later John put on a record and went upstairs to lie on the bed leaning on one elbow, gazing fondly at Hannah and Ingrid, who was drowsily drawing on a nipple.

"What's that music, my love?" Hannah asked, straining to hear.

"It's the Holberg Suite. Greig again. I listened to this a lot last winter when I was away from you." And he rested his head on Hannah's arm, thinking of the years he had lived without her and wondering how many more they would have together.

Hannah felt the dampness from John's eyes on her arm and she drew him closer.

"Music helps me honour my emotions — with honesty," he said with a sniff. "My dad used to say, 'There's nothing wrong with an honest tear, John, my boy. No reason why women should be left to carry all the feelings — their own and ours too'!"

Hannah brushed her lips across John's temple and kissed his eyes. "You had a wise father," she said.

Later that morning Hannah left Ingrid in Emma's ample arms and strolled with John out to the Point. Climbing close to the peak they turned and looked back at the Cove.

"We're one Canada now," John said staunchly.

"From sea to sea. We're in it codstock and barrel!" Hannah replied. "Only time will tell whether we've sold our birthright. But for many of us life has to be better than it was in the past."

Then Hannah's eyes looked down at their shadows on the rough, grey granite. When John followed her gaze and saw that their shadows stretched toward the cemetery, he put an arm around Hannah and gently turned her toward the remainder of the climb to the peak of the Point.

Up on the pinnacle the wind drove Hannah's hair behind her as though drawing back a curtain to present her face, radiant and sunlit, to the world. John brushed his lips across her hair and whispered in her ear, "Now the shadows are all behind us."

They stood beside each other like two keepers of a flame burning unwaveringly between them, untouched even by the force of the ocean winds. Hannah gazed into John's clear blue eyes, their brilliance intensified by the sunswept sea and sky. Gently she framed his face with her hands.

"When we face the sunlight, my love, the shadows will surely fall behind us."

Epilogue

And then what happened? a voice from the circle of those gathered around the fireside would ask the teller of tales. And then what happened?

In the years that followed their marriage, Hannah and John continued to enjoy a delightful and loving closeness. They did have their occasional differences, one of which arose over the matter of lighting, for Hannah disdained the brassy brilliance of John's electric lights. Often she turned off a lamp here and there, preferring the gentle wattage of dusk or dawn, unless they were both reading, an interest they shared with a passion.

Amiably John would take her face in his hands and say, "I think you just miss the little oil lamps of Steadman's Cove!"

Then with a gentle smile Hannah would counter, "Well, my love, is anyone going to do an operation up here tonight?" And often the matter was settled with love and a cluster of candles.

As often as possible John, Hannah and little Ingrid revisited Steadman's Cove to catch up on the news of the Spekes, the Hensons and their other friends in the village. But John and Hannah also travelled far beyond the Cove. And once they visited Sweden, where Hannah gazed nostalgically from high fiordic heights toward her beloved native Newfoundland.

Daniel married Mary Williams and with their three cheery children they worked together to create a centre whose crafts were exported all over North America.

Ingrid Weatherton grew to be tall and fair like her mother. While she was studying art in New York, she married a professor of music. One day, in a moment of quiet exchanges with Daniel, Ingrid made Daniel deeply happy when she said that it was as much from him as from their parents that she had learned a lesson. "You showed me, Danny, that it's from the family you learn to love and care about people. And I know that the more perfect the love, the more complete a person becomes. Thank you for teaching me that."

Almost every summer Ingrid and her husband travelled north to the Bight to share their art and music with people gathered in Hannah's libraries now springing up along the coast and glowing like the warm hearths she dreamed they would be.

Will Speke married a classmate and they practised along-side John, sharing consultations and often seeking his wisdom.

It was John's idea that the Simpson Library at the Bight should also bear an acknowledgement to Hannah. And so he arranged with Belle to have a handsome plaque engraved with a quotation he knew Hannah loved for its depth and subtlety. The words were written by an earlier Hannah:

"The world needs not so much to be told
as to be reminded."
— Hannah More, 1745-1833

May 2011

About the Author

Robina Salter is an award-winning science writer whose articles reflect her skill for unfolding depth and detail. Her first stories were published when she was still a high school student.

Her career as a writer developed while she worked as a public health nurse in the mining communities of northern Ontario. Later she worked with her husband in northern Newfoundland among the people whom she continues to admire and respect.

Mrs. Salter has written short stories for children and adults, and science articles for numerous publications. She has also taught creative writing, lectured and worked as a medical editor. *Hannah* is her first novel.